Follow the Child

of related interest

Bereaved Parents and their Continuing Bonds
Love after Death
Catherine Seigal
ISBN 978 1 78592 326 5
eISBN 978 1 78450 641 4

Helping Children and Adolescents Think about Death, Dying and Bereavement
Marian Carter
ISBN 978 1 78592 011 0
eISBN 978 1 78450 255 3

FOLLOW THE CHILD

Planning and Having the Best
End-of-Life Care for Your Child

SACHA LANGTON-GILKS

Jessica Kingsley *Publishers*
London and Philadelphia

First published in 2018
by Jessica Kingsley Publishers
73 Collier Street
London N1 9BE, UK
and
400 Market Street, Suite 400
Philadelphia, PA 19106, USA

www.jkp.com

Library of Congress Cataloging in Publication Data
A CIP catalog record for this book is available from the Library of Congress

British Library Cataloguing in Publication Data
A CIP catalogue record for this book is available from the British Library

ISBN 978 1 78592 346 3
eISBN 978 1 78450 680 3

For DD, Tessa, Rupert, Tom, Ella, Rosie,
Keisha, Asher, Keir, Ryan, Callum, Stephen,
Maddy, Adam, Kaine, Kimberley, Ellie, Skye
and everyone who loved and cared for them

It is not growing like a tree
In bulk doth make Man better be;
Or standing long an oak, three hundred year,
To fall a log at last, dry, bald, and sere:
A lily of a day
Is fairer far in May,
Although it fall and die that night –
It was the plant and flower of light.
In small proportions we just beauties see;
And in short measures life may perfect be.

Ben Jonson (1573–1637)

Asher Chmiel, 'Ambassador
of Happiness'

Callum David Miller 'Puds'
6th August 2005 – 24th July 2014
My inspiration, my hero

Keir Michael Henry (Lapland 2005)

DD in his element

Ryan 'Ry'

Contents

Acknowledgements

My incredibly patient, loving family: Toby, Holly, Rufus, Mum, Giorgio, Alannah, Marcus, Tessa, Theo, Ruth and Suzy. Holly and Rufus have been particularly supportive, and without their involvement I could not in good conscience have included details of their reactions. Then godparents came in for a lot of extra duties, especially Natalia, Buffy and John, Jonathan and Ginny. Friends were the rock beneath our foundations and there are too many to thank here, but Penny, Emma, Nou, Nikki and Wai Man, Mattie, Bill, Izz, Sian, Julia, Caro, Victoria and Damaris went to infinity and beyond!

I would never have persisted with this book were it not for the positive reaction of Keisha's parents, Zoe and Martin Ranger, who were present with her at my first talk on DD's end-of-life care. They have set up a beautiful holiday home for bereaved families (https://en-gb.facebook.com/keishasblessing).

My most enormous thanks for the generosity of these remarkable mothers and their families in sharing such difficult memories with me for this book: Theresa Chmiel, Alison Jones, Jane Green, Michelle Tonge, Kelly Smith, Sarah Walton, Sally Hall and Zoe Bojelian. It could not have happened without them and their wonderful children.

Carol, our district nurse; Dr Emms, our family's GP, but also Dr Patterson who introduced the vital Gold Standards Framework End of Life Care training into our GP practice.

Dr Gary Nicolin and the team at Southampton and Salisbury Hospitals, especially Hayley who used to come out to DD at home and at school, and Pippa Chesterfield, our specialist palliative care nurse.

Martin Edwards, Chief Executive, Julia's House in Dorset, whose support, encouragement and patient answering of emails, ideas and reading of early drafts were essential.

Dr Lynda Brook, paediatric palliative consultant at Alder Hey Children's Hospital, Liverpool, who read the draft as it went to the publishers and sent invaluable feedback. In the US, I am indebted to Jori Bogetz MD, Assistant Clinical Professor of Pediatrics, Site Director Hospice and Palliative Medicine Fellowship, Integrated Pain and Palliative Care Program (IP3) at UCSF Benioff Children's Hospital University of California, San Francisco – I would never have unearthed an ACP for the US without her help.

Professor Julia Verne, epidemiology unit at Public Health England, to whom I'm indebted for the figures on place of death for children and young people; Professor Keri Thomas, Gold Standards Framework and a heroine of mine for her work on end-of-life care; Professor Bridget Johnston, Florence Nightingale Professor of Nursing and WeEOLC Twitter network.

Rebecca Riley, wonder nurse – adult (RGN), children's (RSCN) and district nurse (DN), whose past experience has included: children and young people's hospice director/lead officer; Together for Short Lives' transition coordinator; Macmillan nurse, Practitioner Health Lecturer in Children and Young People's Palliative Care at the University of Nottingham (2009–2016). Becca is a life coach and person-centred planning practitioner; currently working as a Clinical Associate for Gold Standards Framework (GSF) and a Specialist Advisor in EOL care for Care Quality Commission (CQC). I cannot believe how lucky I am to have had her help and of Rachel Tyler's and Sherelle Ramus' family experience in the Patient-Centred Planning resource.

Theresa's social worker, Jennifer Holler, and Asher's paediatrician, Dr Rex Northup MD, at their hospital were incredibly helpful feeding back on the book from a US standpoint. Her funeral director, Tanner Morris, also kindly checked US details for me. Blyth Lord, founder and Executive Director of the Courageous Parents Network (CPN) in the US, whose daughter Cameron died of Tay-Sachs disease, has also been incredibly supportive.

Suzanne Gwynn (RN) – my US wonder nurse and founder/ CEO of Ladybug House, the children's hospice she is trying to get built to deliver palliative and end-of-life services for the Seattle area. I beg anyone reading this in the corporate world to send her regular large cheques to make those children's wishes come true (Suzanne@ladybughouse.org).

Dr Sarah Russell, Head of Policy at Hospice UK; Gary Winson and Tanya at the mortuary at Southampton General Hospital; GOSH Bereavement Team; Caroline Browne, Head of Regulation for the Human Tissue Authority (HTA), Sue Langley, Library and Information Services at East Anglia Children's Hospices; Sarah Lindsell, Rebecca Shortt and the whole team at the Brain Tumour Charity; Together for Short Lives – Julia Hodgson in particular; Sasha Daly at the Teenage Cancer Trust; Sarah Williamson at CLIC Sargent; Nicole Woodyatt at Macmillan End of Life Care; the British Paramedic Association; Southampton's (Hampshire) Coroner's Office.

Preface

Being able to give my 16-year-old son David – DD as we called him – a good death at home, surrounded by his family and adored pets, will be the greatest achievement of my life. Four years on from his deathday, it remains a huge consolation in my grief to know the last thing I did for my firstborn was exactly what he wanted and needed.

No one wants to talk about end of life, and they usually mean their own or their parents'; it's almost inconceivable it would have to be about your child. They are the most painful conversations I hope I ever have to have. I dreaded and detested them, but you will have to trust me when I say that, looking back, I understand that I *needed* those conversations: I had faced my fears about what was going to happen to our child, and the information I had gained had given me some control, some reassurance, where before I had felt only terrified powerlessness.

At first I was asked to speak about our experience to parents facing end-of-life care for their child. I agreed after the Brain Tumour Charity told me that feedback from parents showed they felt they were given no information and were isolated. I know some friends thought me weird for talking and writing about death, but I love my son as much as any mother, and they have not been there and realised that the worst thought of all was to let my brave child down and make him suffer unnecessarily.

I know it's ironic, given that I and other mothers are talking about the death of our children, but this little book is about *life* because death is not a medical condition. Illness and death do not define my child or the other children you will meet inside

this book; it's *how they live* that defined them. As Stephen Sutton
so beautifully put it shortly before he died of cancer, aged 19:

> I don't see the point of measuring life in terms of time any more.
> I would rather measure it in terms of what I actually achieve. I'd
> rather measure it in terms of making a difference.[1]

---

1   *Contact Magazine*, Issue 64, Autumn 2014, Children's Cancer and Leukaemia Group
     (CCLG), www.cclg.org.uk/write/MediaUploads/Contact%20magazine/1%20Magazine
     %20pdfs/Contact_64.pdf.

INTRODUCTION

This book is, I hope, a form of self-help book because it's aiming to inform, overturn misinformation and be practical. Reassurance and empowerment through information are my aims. I hope it is helpful to parents, the health professionals and friends supporting them, and also the young people themselves who want information, which is why I write you/your child.

This book is *not*:

...a medical textbook, because I'm not a doctor. I have no doctors or health professionals in my immediate family. This is a totally un-medical book by someone who took six months to be able to say the name of the drug Levomapromazine (one of the anti-sickness drugs DD took), let alone all the 'otomies', 'itises' and 'ectomies' spouted by our son's medical team. Like many 21st-century First World mothers, I have several part-time jobs that make for an unpredictable everything – income and timetable: singing teacher, children's choir director, gardener, writer and cook. I am the Lead Champion for the Brain Tumour Charity's HeadSmart campaign, which seeks to reduce the diagnosis time for children and young people's brain tumours in the UK (it still takes much too long).

...a 'journey'. I freely admit I have an aversion to this word which I can't entirely explain. I think it's something to do with it making it sound as if this experience is a personal growth exercise. I know a lot of people find it a very helpful word.

...a religious, healing sort of book, because I'm not religious. This is unfortunate as I feel I would have been able to cope a lot better within the rituals and framework that a religion supplies on the subject of death. To give you context for Chapter 6 (Celebration), my family are in various stages of lapsed Church of England (Protestant). We lamely uphold the broad outlines of the Christian year and both the state primary and secondary schools locally, where our children attend and I teach, are Church of England. DD became fascinated by Buddhism through his friendship with Wai Man, a Buddhist who's a great family friend. In this he was following the example of my Irish maternal grandmother who converted to Buddhism in the 1950s. Meditating was without doubt the most useful tool DD had during his five years from diagnosis to death, especially when dealing with bumped operations and severe stress. I tried meditating but am too impatient. Gardening and singing work better for me.

...concerned with alternative medicine. It does stray into complementary if you count meditating, massage, food and relaxation techniques (basically anything that would complement rather than counter the management of symptoms and wouldn't worry our doctors). It is guided by evidence and data from professionals as much as possible. No leap of faith is required!

...about bereavement in the sense of loss *after* death. It is about loss *before* death (anticipatory grief). If you're looking for help coping with the Mount Everest of grief after a child has died, there are lots of books out there written by bereaved parents.[1]

...a list of available palliative care services, as they vary nationally and internationally. I've been shocked to discover that the US has only two children's hospices nationally for roughly 500,000 children with life-threatening conditions,

---

1   The charity Child Bereavement UK has superb information on all aspects.

compared with 54 in the UK. Their insurance companies baulk at covering what is an expensive service compared with adults' palliative and hospice care programmes, when in fact there is data showing it's considerably cheaper to have children early in comprehensive in-home paediatric palliative hospice care (PP/HC).[2] This is reflected in the language used in the US: there, hospice is 'service/insurance benefit' in a few areas, whereas hospice is a 'place' here in the UK. It means that US families, particularly in rural areas, have little or no access to palliative support and can end up spending months, sometimes years, in hospital hundreds of miles from their communities. Adults in the US can access hospice care, but it's rare for children and teenagers, which I find incomprehensible given the physical, mental and financial damage to families left without support. I have been incredibly lucky to have been put in touch with a mum in the US, Theresa Chmiel, and her family's experience gives an international aspect to what is otherwise a book from a British perspective. She also has approached decisions from the foundations of religious faith (see Chapters 3 and 6), which makes me feel less guilty for my omissions. I try my best to be clear about the differences between the UK and US systems and stick to their own spellings – for example, paediatric (UK) and pediatric (US).

In the UK, palliative care services for children and young people, though plentiful compared with the US, are currently a postcode lottery, which I find entirely unacceptable for the 49,000 children and young people affected by one or more of around 390 different life-threatening or life-shortening conditions requiring support. One of the main reasons for this is that although we have a hospice network, we lack managed

---

2   Gans, D., Kominski, G.F., Roby, D.H., Diamant, A.L. *et al.* (2012) 'Better outcomes, lower costs: Palliative care program reduces stress, costs of care for children with life-threatening conditions.' Policy Brief, UCLA Center for Health Policy Research, PB2012–3, 1–8; Gans, D., Hadler, M.W., Chen, X., Wu, S.H. *et al.* (2016) 'Cost analysis and policy implications of a pediatric palliative care program.' *Journal of Pain and Symptom Management 52*, 3, 329–335.

clinical networks (MCNs) to link everything together, which is why the UK's National Institute for Health and Care Excellence (NICE) has recommended they be put in place. If you need a list of services in the UK, may I immediately direct you to the website of the national charity Together for Short Lives (see Resources) where you will discover the range of support in your area.

...about palliative care as a whole. This book is focussed on end-of-life care – a small, albeit vital part of the job description of palliative services. According to the Royal College of Paediatric and Child Health, in 2012 over 3,000 babies died before age 1 and 2,000 children and young people died between the ages of 1 and 19.[3] In the US, it is 41,881 children (0–19 years), of which 23,215 are children under one year.[4] In adults, end of life is usually defined as the last year of life, but then death, like birth, is very unpredictable in its details. This is even truer for children and young people who, thanks to continuing medical improvements and the dedicated care of their families, seem to have the most fantastic and inspiring ability to prove their doctors' predictions wrong and live far longer than expected with incredibly complex conditions. No good data exists yet on how to recognise that a child is dying, as unbelievable as that sounds.[5] Their end of life is only said to last longer than adults'; in the absence of better data, that currently means longer than a year. So, for the purposes of this book, let's just say when the parents and the medical team know that

3   *Why Children Die: Death in infants, children and young people in the UK Part A* (2014) Wolfe I., Macfarlane A., Donkin A., Marmot M. and Viner R., on behalf of Royal College of Paediatrics and Child Health, National Children's Bureau and British Association for Child and Adolescent Health, https://www.rcpch.ac.uk/sites/default/files/page/Death%20in%20infants,%20children%20and%20young%20people%20in%20the%20UK.pdf.

4   National Center for Health Statistics 2014, www.cdc.gov/nchs/fastats/child-health.htm.

5   See NICE, 'End of life care for infants, children and young people with life-limiting conditions: planning and management', NICE guideline: short version, draft for consultation, 2016, www.nice.org.uk/guidance/ng61/documents/short-version-of-draft-guideline, pp.37–39.

something has changed and the incurable disease now has the upper hand. This variability is why I include the word 'roughly' in the titles of Chapters 3 and 4.

...just about end-of-life care for children and young people with cancer, although that is the biggest killer disease of children over the age of two and it killed DD. I have had the great privilege to receive help with this book in the form of spoken and written testimony from several mothers whose children had different diseases: Theresa, whom I've just mentioned, whose son Asher had Dandy-Walker malformation/syndrome, cerebral palsy, seizures and a wide range of other musculoskeletal and congenital abnormalities, diagnosed at birth; Michelle Tonge, who lives in the north of Bolton and whose son, Keir, was diagnosed with metachromatic leukodystrophy aged five; Alison Jones, from Shropshire, whose son, Ryan, was diagnosed aged three with Krabbe's leukodystrophy; and Jane Green in Essex, a student paediatric nurse, whose son Callum was deprived of oxygen at birth. I received spoken testimony from many other families, mentioned in the dedication or acknowledgements. I've also quoted mothers and siblings featured in a book supporting Children's Hospice South West and Jessie May Children's Hospice at Home.[6] There are also parents who lost a baby. Parents often know in advance of the birth that they are going to lose their baby, either as a stillborn or newborn (neonate) and it's shocking how many deaths occur each year in this way.[7]

...just about a death at home in the community. DD wanted to be at home, so that's where he died, but I also wanted to include stories in which a family went to a hospice or stayed

---

6   *Lives Worth Living: Fifteen Stories of Exceptional Children Whose Short Lives Left a Lasting Legacy*, written by their families, with Janet Cotter (Southgate Publishers, 2014).

7   In England in 2012, 3558 babies were stillborn and a further 1990 babies died in the neonatal period. National Perinatal Epidemiology Unit, University of Oxford, 'Listening to parents after stillbirth or the death of their baby after birth', www.npeu.ox.ac.uk/listeningtoparents.

in hospital, so that you could hear about a variety of different settings. Both Keir, aged 13, and eight-year-old Callum died at home having been in hospital until a few days before. Ryan was just six when he died in Hope House Children's Hospice near Oswestry. Over in Florida, Theresa's son Asher died in hospital aged 12.

Having said all that, it's now time for a bit more of our family background, so you can see the point at which DD, my husband, Toby, and I reached what I call 'The Difficult Conversation' and the effective start to this book. DD had an aggressive brain tumour – the biggest child and young people's cancer killer, accounting for roughly ten children or young people's deaths every month in the UK. He was diagnosed with a medulloblastoma in Southampton General Hospital in October 2007, aged 11, when his little sister, Holly, was just five and his brother, Rufus, nine. At that point the science and medicine of the day gave him an excellent 75% chance of being eventually cured, but he needed to live ten years before he earned that very hard five-letter word. We were scared but very optimistic, and our medical team was world-class.

Over the five years of DD's illness, during periods of intensive treatment or complication Toby and I would take shifts of three days in hospital with DD (the maximum stretch, I discovered, that I can cope with sleep deprivation over a long period) and then three days off with Rufus and Holly at home. This meant the children were always with one of us. We regularly used the CLIC Sargent parent hostel as a vital halfway house when things were not medically clear-cut, and it meant that special days, such as birthdays, could be fun for everyone, as Holly and Rufus could stay in the hostel with us. We both tried to work, as much as DD's epic fluctuations in health over the years allowed, but clearly it was sporadic. Life insurance on our mortgage covered expenses the first year, but then we were effectively rescued by a consortium of our community and friends worldwide who supplemented the UK government's carers' allowance. We can never thank our friends enough.

My mother – my father having died of cancer a decade earlier – would move in at home if DD needed surgery, and then both Toby and I would be with him in hospital. The round trip to hospital from our rural corner of Dorset was roughly an hour each way in good weather, without traffic, so I think we all know what that means in the UK – vast quantities of money spent over five years on petrol and parking and hours of stressful driving with a vomiting, critically ill passenger. (In the US that would be regarded as very local, which is a terrifying thought.) The vomiting was the result of the post-operative meningitis he contracted 24 hours after being first discharged or the six weeks of daily radiotherapy to his whole brain and spine, the curative chemotherapy that was a total of 15 months long, the later chemotherapy that was another five months long preceding a stem cell rescue, or the 11 brain procedures in two and a half years ranging from nine hours to 40 minutes, resulting from hydro- or hypocephalus (in non-medic terms, brain pressure issues as a result of late diagnosis at the start). I'm speeding through all this so that you see that DD had many near-death episodes in those five years, but up until the Difficult Conversation, we still had a 30–50% chance (depending on whose data you chose to believe) that the stem cell rescue would eventually cure him. He needed to have lived five years to find out if it had worked.

As we arrive at the Difficult Conversation, DD is now 16; he is particularly close to his little sister, now nine, who worships the air he breathes. He is the same size he was at 11 (luckily he was tall for his age at that point), as the radiotherapy has damaged his pituitary gland. This resulted in an additional diagnosis of life-threatening Addison's disease and he is undergoing growth hormone treatment to put him through puberty. He's doing his GCSEs this summer and is predicted top grades. Holly, seven years younger than her big brother, has very successfully managed to give him back the childhood that extreme cancer treatment effectively takes. She is utterly uninterested in the fact that he has cancer and treats him accordingly, which he adores.

For example, very cross with him one morning for taking her DS game, she shouts, 'Go and have some more chemotherapy!' After a shocked silence, everyone roared with laughter because we all knew it was outrageous. (This is perhaps the point I should warn you about the Langton-Gilks family's sense of humour, much prized within the family as a genetic trait but clearly horrifying to many outside it.)

Rufus is 14 and getting on much better with his older brother, who has freely admitted 'cancer has made me much nicer'. DD had been awful to his sibling when they were little. Pure sibling jealousy due to Rufus being a blonde cherub who could curb his few tantrums on sight of a chocolate biscuit (unlike DD), was placid (unlike DD) and naturally gifted at sport, music, friends (like DD) and therefore had no great difficulty in keeping up with his brother. DD and I had spent what I shall describe as a 'sustained campaign' in the toddler trenches, as I had no idea how to cope with a child who was so furious and I was doing all the childcare. I leaned on him and the curve was steep, poor child. We finally arrived at understanding when DD was just over four and, as a result, he and I were particularly close. None of this had endeared him to his father.

Toby's own learning curve with his eldest coincided with the cancer diagnosis and was therefore even steeper. He was on shift the night after the first massive, nine-hour brain surgery as I was unsafe, having been up 48 hours straight. Until this moment my husband had never had to make any decisions about medicines for the children and he was terrified. I had taken them to all their childhood injections and decided what to do throughout all the usual plethora of childhood illnesses, as he was working. That night was transformative for my husband. He found that with the medical team's help he could do it: he could care for his son and he was a good dad. There's nothing like staring at the bank of machinery keeping your child alive for re-evaluating everything about your life, and my husband determined he would pull out of his work depression and his anger after the loss of both of his parents in the previous few years, and enjoy his children and life. Toby's main job then was as a composer of television music, but the business was in a desperate state due to the arrival of scores of digital channels and the subsequent collapse of commissioning budgets. He now teaches music in the local prison and a few schools, with composing remaining a badly paid but creatively rewarding sideline.

I mustn't leave out the pets, so vital to our family's sense of wellbeing. They don't know DD has cancer and therefore carry on doing what they do. One Golden Retriever, Honeybun (witty and interesting pet names elude us), who belongs to (and only answers to) Toby and Rufus, and two cats. DD's cat was his sixth birthday present and she is generally described as having special needs and appears to be deaf. His real passion are the bees. They belong to Dave, who is teaching DD to become an apiarist. This is a massive success in the sense that DD's stem cell rescue has left him utterly exhausted and unable to do sports or be at our local school with his mates as much as he would like (which would be all the time). He is fascinated by the bees and by science generally, particularly anything to do with the environment. I realise just how lucky we are to live in a beautiful part of the country, in an unspoilt environment that includes a pair of kingfishers, a barn owl and tawny owls (another DD obsession), woodpeckers (Green and Greater Spotted), goldfinches, buzzards, jays, cuckoos, thrushes and myriad seasonal moths and butterflies. The insects sup off the nectar of wildflowers and trees alongside a brook that runs into an old mill race, where we swim in the summer months. These natural gifts feed my ill child in every sense of the word and lead to interests in flying birds of prey, bonsai trees, drawing, pottery, cookery and an ambition to go to university to read one of the sciences. They are the key to his quality of life.

At this point, in May 2012, I'm 44 years old and I've become very good at managing a highly unpredictable life and asking for and getting a lot of help, but let's not kid ourselves: I'm hanging on by my fingernails. I have a constant feeling I'll never catch my tail and I'm doing everything very badly. I'm also deeply anxious about my eldest child. He should have been slowly getting stronger after the horrendous stem cell rescue a year before, but I have this sense that everything's just getting harder for him and I can't pinpoint why. He's technically in remission and everyone's very pleased but…

I finally take him in desperation to a GP who has also trained in complementary medicine to see if there's anything else I can do to try to boost DD's immune system. He prescribes some supplements. But then on the way home DD asks me which route we're taking back; I reply and then a minute later he asks exactly the same question. There is nothing in the world like the void of terror, the sickening lurch and impact of pressure that hits the chest when your body responds to an understanding before your brain has even formed a sentence to itself: I knew then. I went into denial for over a month, as I had nothing else to go on and we had danced with death so many times already. I made excuses to myself: I was just tired, I was hyper-alert, why wouldn't I worry, he was fine and everyone including Toby said so…

…until fateful Friday. DD set off as usual for his hour-long Taekwondo class in the village with Holly. I was making supper. Half an hour later, I hear footsteps thump up the stairs, a door slam and muffled sobs. He never ever behaved like that. Feeling sick, I went to enquire.

'I couldn't remember what he said in class, I couldn't do it, my balance…' DD sobbed. 'Go away!'

The best scenario at this point would be that his shunt had blocked and that was affecting his balance, but he didn't have a headache and he knew shunt symptoms well.

You know you're in deep, deep trouble when you're *hoping* your child needs more brain surgery. I rang the hospital and said we were coming in first thing Monday morning when the whole team would be there unless he suddenly deteriorated; he would need an immediate MRI scan.

NB. You can read the chapters in any order, as you need, or you can just hurl the book in the bin as I did with a fat How-to-care-for-your-baby book when DD was a few months old.

Chapter 1

THE DIFFICULT CONVERSATION(S)[1] PART I

AN INCURABLE DIAGNOSIS

The diagnosis is the shocking bit and it can arrive in many different ways. I've used the word 'incurable' instead of 'terminal' because it can be decades between an incurable diagnosis and it becoming terminal, the end of life, depending on the disease and a whole host of other factors. It could also, unfortunately, be hours, with immense pressure to make life-changing decisions which often cannot be reversed. So I've named the conversations Part I and Part II, but they obviously overlap. The reason I say conversation with an plural 's' on the end is because it is often a series of conversations with your medical team, lots of bits of information, whilst you try to process what is happening to your family. This is especially true if one parent is more ready to cope with the conversation than the other or if the parents are separated or divorced and relations are already fraught.[2]

You could be told in an acute care setting such as a paediatric intensive care unit (PICU), at accident and emergency, or at a paediatric outpatient clinic. You could be told at a routine pregnancy scan that your child has a life-shortening condition or in the early hours, days or years of their life by a paediatrician

---

1   If you're a health care professional (HCP), call it the Important Conversation so you're not tempted to put it off!

2   The CCLG booklet *Facing the Death of Your Child: Suggestions and Help for Families, Before and Afterwards* has advice for divided families (see Resources for details).

or disease specialist. You could be told by an oncologist at the outset of a cancer diagnosis where it has spread and is not curable. Or you might have our path, where we had the expectation that DD would survive and then it changes and you have to hear that the cancer is no longer curable. Whichever way, it is agonisingly hard. You are instantly plunged into grief for the life, the future, you thought you/your child and, by extension, the whole family would have – anticipatory grief, as it is called (see Chapter 3).

The main things standing in the way of good communication in these conversations for both parents and their doctors are fear, denial and how you define hope. I'm going to tackle each to unravel what is otherwise a knotted mess of emotion complicated by public misunderstanding of what palliative care actually means. Know now that having these conversations does not mean giving up on your child and losing hope; quite the reverse.

TOP TIP

Take someone into the meeting with you who: knows your family well; you trust implicitly; can be an objective listener and note-taker – neighbour, auntie, godparent, friend. They can also drive you home.

FEAR

No passion so effectually robs the mind of all its powers of acting and reasoning as fear.

Edmund Burke (1757)

It's important to say first that, like births, all deaths are different, unique, and obviously reflect the infinite variety of medical, personal, emotional, spiritual, mental and financial circumstances of the particular individual or family. People are generally scared about *how* you die, the process of getting there, especially if they have no experience of being with a person when they die, and this, of course, is magnified exponentially when you're frightened on your child's behalf. Toby and I both had the advantage of having been with our fathers when they died – death was not an unknown. But I realise it's important to separate the fear of how your child will die from the fear of the loss, of that emotional pain. I was told by a mother whose child died at home a couple of years before DD that 'the death was okay' – they stop breathing, their suffering ends. That was a huge reassurance, mad as that must sound. I remember thinking if she can do it, so can I, and I'm telling you in this book: *if I can do it, so can you*, wherever you are: we're a chain of mothers, of fathers, holding our hands to the next one. *You are not alone.* It's the loss that is not okay, but that's another subject (bereavement).

People also fear that they won't now have enough time to do what they want. It is no different for young people. I know I had all of those fears merged into one huge *How will I cope? How can I do this? I don't want to; I can't.* The answer lies in the title of this book: *Follow the Child.* Don't think that your child will think what you are thinking about death – they often have little experience of it apart from perhaps losing a loved pet; children have to be taught to fear. I learned to listen to exactly what DD wanted to do that day and my job was to figure out how to make it happen with our medical team. I was air traffic control faced with a stack of planes waiting to land and I learned just to identify which was the most urgent and land that first, not try to land everything together!

The foremost explorer, Sir Ranulph Fiennes, managed to conquer his acute fear of heights and climb Mount Everest by shutting down his imagination and doing exactly what his guide told him which was: *do not look down* and *do not imagine what it would be like to look down!* The equivalent for parents is to shut down your imagination, do exactly what your child tells you and *don't think you won't cope* and *do not imagine what it will be like when your child dies.*

DENIAL

What I've just asked you to do is not the same as pretending your child will not die from their disease = denial. Denial is fear using its main weapon. I had to learn to face up to what was happening, not bury it. I freely admit that denial can be very useful as a temporary distraction, a holding pattern to let you catch your breath, but if it never evolves beyond that, it can be devastating after the inevitable death because shock has been added to the loss. I look back and compare myself in denial to someone watching the national weather forecast, seeing a hurricane warning with threat to life and property, and saying to myself, it won't hit here; it'll hit the neighbours and move on. The result is I don't prepare – clear the drains, protect windows, tie things down – and then when the hurricane does arrive, I'm not only hit but the devastation is much worse than it need have been.

A key understanding for me, in order to tackle denial, is this. You can't make your child's death happen by thinking or talking about it. Death has its own timetable and no doctor will ever be able to tell you for certain when your child will die – in other words, a prognosis for an incurable condition will always be an educated guess. Here is a mother, Julia, reflecting on talking about her child Kimberley's funeral *with her* in advance; having done so, they were able to reassure her that 'her wishes would be respected':

> I understand now that...doesn't mean that you're chancing fate or that you're accepting that it is going to happen. *If you are honest with yourself* you know it will happen, sooner than you want, but you have to live with that knowledge. Many people fear that if you're discussing it, you are making it more real and perhaps making it come sooner. Others take the opposite view and think that by not focussing on it, it makes the inevitable disappear, almost. With hindsight I realise neither of these is true.[3]

---

3   *Lives Worth Living: Fifteen Stories of Exceptional Children Whose Short Lives Left a Lasting Legacy*, p.92 (my italics).

If you adopt the 'don't you dare talk to us about it, we'll take it as it comes, thank you', the guaranteed downside is *avoidable* crises (note the plural). Children can become seriously ill seriously fast, and from a stable situation, a panicked emergency call is a heartbeat away. This is so frightening for everybody. I knew this because it happened to my mum managing my dad's end of life at home. Also, we had had so many crises with DD over the five years; I was determined not to repeat this with his end-of-life care, especially with Holly and Rufus mostly on their summer holidays. With good planning, we succeeded.

THE BYSTANDER EFFECT AND THE NEED FOR CLARITY

The main thing is to have clarity in these Difficult Conversations, so that you can make informed choices in the best interest of or with your child. If you don't accept or it's not clear your child will die, you won't be linked to all the services that can improve their quality of life and that of the entire family and could ultimately enable them to live longer (see below). I know it's much easier said than done, because it's not just the parents who are scared of these difficult conversations.

Doctors are trained to save lives and therefore find it very hard to talk about death; it's much easier for a disease specialist to talk about 'fixing' a specific medical problem and ignore the elephant in the room. The doctor is scared that they will make parents 'more upset' by being clear that this disease will shorten their child's life. The phrase I have often heard from doctors is: 'You have to respect that some people don't want to know... They can get very angry when you tell them.' My response is: Who would *want* to know? Want has nothing to do with it; I needed to know so that we could be prepared in every sense. I don't think I could have been 'more upset' either – I was already on DEFCON 1 in terms of emotions. Anger in this situation is nothing to be ashamed of, and doctors should expect it from parents as a normal part of processing what is happening. If the doctor doubts they can handle it honestly, they should make sure they have a professional there who is good and practised at it. Otherwise, it's too tempting for them to talk about interventions/procedures they can do without ever discussing whether they should and what effect these will have on the quality of life of that child and family.

In reality, what can often happen is the doctor can be vague and it feels like a weird over-sensitivity that all adds up to a very convoluted conversation. They might use euphemisms like 'letting them go' or 'go and enjoy time together whilst you can – go on holiday', or add more and more medical bad news, say that your child is 'very poorly', use words like 'futile', 'inappropriate', 'not beneficial', or say that treatment is not working or not going to work. They may not actually say the hard words 'incurable' or the 'Ds' of 'death' and 'die', and hope that the parents understand that's what they mean. However, it's like Voldemort in the Harry Potter books: not saying it makes it scarier because that pressure in the air of something unsaid leaves space for fear, which makes everything worse.

Health professionals acknowledge this problem of lack of clarity and call it the bystander effect: everyone hopes someone else is going step in, take responsibility and be really clear to the family, which then starts the end-of-life planning process, but no one does – parents are often judged 'not ready' for the information. Parents usually don't want to understand; we can't because it's so painful and so we don't. It all means that clarity around the child's inevitable death is put off and off, sometimes until literally a few days from the death when it can no longer be denied. If you are only told clearly your child is going to die a couple of days before, when in fact the doctors knew months previously that this was inevitable given their disease, it is very difficult to process and deliver all the choices I'm going to detail in this book, even if they're readily available in your area. I know of families where their child has died in the ambulance that was taking them back home to die because it was left so late.

If you're not sure what is being said, what the diagnosis is and means, ask the health professionals, preferably someone trained in palliative care, until you *do* understand. We will one day arrive at a point where you will never get an incurable diagnosis for your child without one of these palliative professionals being present, but at the moment it tends to be a paediatrician or a specialist in a disease, or a cluster of them if your child has a very complex condition. If your English is not up to complex medical words, ask for a translator. If you can't face it that day, make an appointment for a follow-up.

Remember, there's no such thing as a stupid question, ever.

DEALING WITH THE P-WORD – PALLIATIVE

NB. If you're a paediatrician or disease specialist giving a diagnosis and making this referral, please make sure your young patient/parents understand this; otherwise, they won't be able to hear you because they misunderstand 'palliative' as 'I am/my child is dying *now*'.

I need to say right away: palliative care is *not* just end-of-life care and it does *not* mean stopping treatment and therefore giving up and letting someone die. It does not mean doctors are suddenly doing nothing and stopping caring for you/your child; quite the reverse. (It is anyway illegal to actively end a patient's life – euthanasia.) The actual dying bit, when a body is shutting down and the organs failing, is, to me, the last few days, which leaves a lot of time – it can be many years – when your child is seriously ill but still managing to do so many things. Therefore, if you are given a palliative referral, in most cases you are *not* being told you/they are dying now – palliative doctors are 'not the death and dying squad', as Theresa so brilliantly put it. Jane Green was actually training to become an adult nurse when Callum was born and she admits she thought she understood what palliative care was, but then when he was referred to the palliative care team, 'I thought that a diagnosis had been made and no one was telling me that Callum was dying'.[4] I myself, like all the other parents on the children's cancer ward, was terrified of the P-word. There was a silence around the words 'palliative' and 'they're going home' and in that vacuum of information it only meant *die*.

This misunderstanding about what palliative care means then extends to what people think a hospice is. They think it means their child is near death and that a hospice is only for dying. This means families delay going through fear and then are not linked to all the services that can help. In fact, a hospice is for care from the point of diagnosis/eligibility – that is, when the condition becomes life-shortening or life-threatening – until death, however many days/weeks/months/years that may be. All the mothers I've spoken to said that getting to their hospice and realising what it offered to the whole family was the best thing they ever did.

There is now good data out there[5] to show that having access early to a palliative team can enable you to live a good deal longer than if you do not (admittedly this research is in adults, but the principle is the same). I definitely want to have a conversation that might mean my child doesn't have to do the chemotherapy but lives significantly longer!

Palliative care can be referred to as comfort or supportive or selective care/treatments, but for me that gives a passive impression. Its intention is 'to alleviate the harms produced by illness and disabilities'.[6] Far from being passive and inactive, palliative care can entail a lot of medical intervention, including surgery, if that's what it takes to allow you/your child to continue

---

4   Jane says these are now called symptom management teams, reflecting a large part of what they do.

5   In *Being Mortal: Medicine and What Matters in the End* (Picador, 2015), Atul Gawande cites evidence from a trial at Massachusetts General Hospital in 2010 where a group of end-stage lung cancer patients (stage 4) given palliative support alongside oncology lived 25% longer, despite most choosing not to do more chemotherapy, than the group that only had oncology (pp.177, 274).

6   Royal College of Paediatrics and Child Health (2015) 'Making decisions to limit treatment in life-limiting and life-threatening conditions in children: A framework for practice', p.16 (see 'A few publications' in the Resources).

doing the things they love. I have not met anyone who already knew this unless they were a health professional. Furthermore, children and young people's palliative care is not mini-adult; they have different needs – a fact often not understood by commissioners and providers of care. Children tend to die from rarer, more complex illnesses which need management over many years (the average length of care for adults in community-based hospice care is currently about 91 days) and they need access to additional social workers, nutritionists, music and art therapists, educational specialists and so on.

Palliative medicine is the branch that manages incurable diseases. Theoretically, I take palliative medicine for my asthma, which is incurable and life-threatening. Palliative care is focussed on the child and their family in a holistic way that is very different to the approach of a doctor and medical team who specialise in a disease. Palliative specialists coordinate and synthesise care across the child's whole team of specialities, professions and care settings, advocating for the family and helping the family to do likewise, enabling the best quality of life for that child every single day. The emphasis is *life*, living but also talking about the possibility of the child's death and what might be helpful for the parents before and after, so the family is prepared (see 'Parallel planning' below). This preparation, this knowledge, neutralises so much fear to free up energy for enjoying life.

I now know that palliative specialists (whether doctors, nurses or care workers) are the health professionals who can tell you what your child *can* do, not just a list of things they can't, or what they can do *for* your child, not just *to* them. I just wish someone had told me this right at the start of DD's diagnosis, even when the odds were that his cancer would be cured; then I wouldn't have been scared of them. Had he survived, we would have needed palliative support anyway for the rest of his life for the life-threatening side-effects of his many treatments.

HOPE

For me, redefining hope is the essence of the Difficult
Conversations with your/your child's doctors and therapists.
We all have hopes and dreams and have them for our children,
but a devastating diagnosis like this means we have to change
them. Facing up to your/your child's death doesn't mean you're
giving up. Hope is not being taken away; you are still being
positive – it's just that you are striving for something different to
cure. 'Hope is the expectation of a good that is yet to be.'[7] The
question is: What do you now hope you/your child can do?
The hope can change every day, but answering will help you see
a future for your child. No one underestimates the difficulty of
this grieving process – it is the kernel of our/parental pain.

I know that for a long time I was not clear in my own mind
between hope and false hope – I did not check that my expectations
were realistic; I was in denial. I think it's particularly difficult if
your child has a disease that has a chance of cure. You want to
believe your child is going to survive, even in the face of obvious
medical evidence to the contrary, and be the one that overcomes
insurmountable odds – it's simultaneously such a powerful
instinct and a big, clear storyline. The media reinforce this idea
all the time, especially with cancer, but I notice they always put
quotation marks around the word miracle: 'Eight-year-old free
of cancer after "miracle" treatment' is a recent example. This is
because the newspaper knows there is no scientific evidence for
the treatment working and the fact the patient is feeling better
could be down to any number of different things; the miracle is
coincidence. The narrative holds that hope, being positive, only
means fighting/battling/surviving and is about denying that the
disease might kill you. It implies that you can be a coward and
a failure – negative – if you don't survive; blame and therefore
shame are piled on to the individual rather than the disease. That
is so unfair and we need make society at large aware of this.

---

7   Sherwin B. Nuland, *How We Die: Reflections on Life's Final Chapter* (Chatto & Windus,
     1993), p.223.

It is only when you've had a chance at a cure for a terrible disease and it has not worked that you learn how cruel this is and come to know the pain of the evil twin of hope – despair. Michelle and her husband had that miracle dangled in front of them after they had met the world-renowned doctor and raised and sent the money, but then it turned out that Keir was not going to qualify for the pioneering research and treatment after all. She says, 'We didn't hope for anything after that'. I remember saying to a close friend after DD's stem cell transplant, 'I don't do hope', and their reaction was to be horrified: 'You can't give up!', 'You've got to feel you've tried everything, right?' and 'You've got to be positive!' It drove me crazy because I didn't mean we had given up and didn't know how to reply, and it just added guilt on top of everything else: DD's cancer came back because I had *failed* to make him be positive enough?

This book has given me the chance to answer. Hope is never small and it is completely personal: one person's lifetime-best achievement might be considered a normal day's activity to someone else. Despair caused by unrealistic expectations is so much worse in my experience than facing the bottom line – death – and being realistic about what you/they can achieve before that happens. The roller-coaster you go on for 'miracle' cures is so exhausting to recover from, to haul the whole family back up from, that it's far safer – if I continue the theme park analogy – for everyone to just go for a lovely swing in the local park! If your child has done every medical intervention available for their disease and it hasn't worked or no longer works and they're exhausted, it is not cowardly or negative or 'giving up' to ask how they would like to spend their time and go and do it. It's also not about me satisfying myself I have tried everything when I could see how much those aggressive treatments made DD suffer; that was selfish of me and not the loving thing to do. This was made worse by my realisation that DD was doing these horrendous treatments in part to please Toby and me. Children tend not to be worrying about themselves; they worry about their parents and their siblings, although they might not show it, and will do anything to please them, even if it means a lot of extra suffering.

Again, doctors can struggle with hope because of their training. The American surgeon Sherwin B. Nuland says in his chapter on 'Hope and the Cancer Patient':

> A young doctor learns no more important lesson than the admonition that he must never allow his patients to lose hope, even when they are obviously dying.[8]

He means that the doctor thinks they should not be honest and tell the patient they are going to die because the doctor has defined hope only as cure. Doctors love fixing things and they hate it when they can't 'do' anything; they think they've failed in some way – which is mad given how desperately they have usually fought to save our children. I feel DD's medical team did the opposite of fail – his quality of life and good death were a triumph because just living well every day with serious disease, even if you die at the end, is 'doing' plenty! You could say palliative care is just a different kind of 'doing' to 'fixing'!

PARALLEL PLANNING

This is just the phrase the doctors use to mean that they talk about and plan end-of-life care with the family right from the start of an incurable diagnosis, whilst obviously hoping that it will not be needed for ages and maybe not at all if a cure suddenly becomes available. Put simply: hoping for the best but preparing for the worst. Done well, it means that care will link up seamlessly and the family will be prepared because you are planning for life and death. Just having a plan helps with the relentless uncertainty. As mum Fiona writes about her daughter, Yasmin:[9]

---

8   *How We Die: Reflections on Life's Final Chapter* (Chatto & Windus, 1993), p.222.
9   *Lives Worth Living: Fifteen Stories of Exceptional Children Whose Short Lives Left a Lasting Legacy*, p.113.

> I knew how important it was for me to know Yasmin could leave us at any time. I wanted [her siblings] to have the same opportunity to do and say all they needed to before she went.

It takes real guts from everyone to keep revisiting the plan as medical circumstances change, as they always do. That's the thing: the plan isn't concrete; it's flexible and adaptive to respond to change in need. However, the need to continue to revisit the plan has been reinforced by reading the stories of families of children with life-shortening and incredibly complex conditions, and seeing this over and over from the parents after the death: 'We never thought that she/he would actually die.' To anyone on the outside, seeing an incredibly sick/disabled child who has an incurable, life-shortening condition, this must sound totally crazy. However, as a parent in that situation, when your family has found joy in unexpected places and your beloved child has defied death on countless occasions, you just don't think it will happen because it's over there – it's *elsewhere*. It's across the mythical River Styx. You therefore are incredibly tempted to put the conversation off because you don't want to think it will happen. And it can happen so fast...

Michelle's doctor, Dan Hindley, a paediatrician, has written a very moving letter published under the title 'Looking after Keir'.[10] He would visit Keir every two months at home, more often if he was needed. Generally, as Keir was stable for ages, he would just briefly review medication and do a ritual 'laying on of stethoscope' and have a chat where Keir would tell jokes! Dr Hindley describes arriving with the first draft of the personal resuscitation plan for Keir a long time before it was needed (he looked after him for nine years in total). He looks back and worries that he was too forward discussing end of life when there were no signs of it, and he that should have given the family more space. However, he continues: 'Another part of me reflects that laying that honest foundation gave a focus and reality to all our discussions since.'

---

10 Letters, *BMJ Supportive and Palliative Care, 4*, 228–229 (2014).

These he describes as follows:

> Every now and then, we would have one of those deep, intense
> and perceptive conversations about what was going to happen,
> whether there was any cure, how long he would last, how he
> was feeling – questions to which I had few answers but to
> which I tried to respond with honesty and the benefit of some
> experience. There was always some relief when I could tweak
> a medication here or involve some useful therapist there but
> probably the conversations over a long period of time were the
> most beneficial strings to my limited bow.

He concludes:

> In the end, given the information and the time and the trusted
> relationships, nearly all families will let us know the best path
> for their individual child.

Sounds like perfect parallel planning to me! Michelle will tell it
from her perspective below.

WHAT YOU CAN DO IF YOU DISAGREE

The most difficult situation for the family is when they
fundamentally disagree with the doctors about how to define
hope, the future, for that child, sometimes to the point that courts
get involved. It can be either way around: the doctors wanting
to do medical interventions when the family doesn't want them
to, or vice versa. I'm including in this parents wanting to keep
a pregnancy which the doctors think they should terminate on
medical grounds. Equally impossible is if the child disagrees
with the family and wants to refuse a treatment and they are
legally held to be competent to make that decision.[11] As if
making decisions in the best interest of the child (best interest

---

11 For the ethical and legal framework for these decisions, see Royal College of Paediatrics
    and Child Health (2015) 'Making decisions to limit treatment in life-limiting and life-
    threatening conditions in children: A framework for practice' (see 'A few publications'
    in the Resources).

decisions) were not ethically and emotionally difficult enough, add to this the frequent complication of divorced couples or even married ones not being equally ready for the conversation but also then disagreeing, as my husband and I certainly did prior to one of DD's many brain surgeries. Toby and I were certainly imbalanced as a couple throughout our first year, with my husband literally unable to speak about what was happening to us, whilst I could only cope by linking and talking to the nurses and other mothers on the ward. It puts enormous stress on marriages, and I can completely imagine the rows we might have had if we had had to face an end-of-life scenario straight away with DD. It can be such hard work to look after each other!

- Tell someone if you can – the Maggie's Centres in support of people with cancer and their families on hospital sites have free counselling available, as do hospices who support families for all life-threatening conditions. Given the lack of hospices in the US, the American Association for Marriage and Family Therapy has state and provincial groups that will be able to help (see Resources). Also do watch the brilliant videos on the Courageous Parents Network (see Resources) such as 'Tending the Marriage: Strengthening Your Parenting Partnership': they have free membership and 24-hour online forums.

- Ask for a meeting on your own. Toby did this with our oncologist and howled tears man to man. (I tended to howl at the nurses.)

- If you're a single parent, you could take someone you trust with you as a fresh pair of ears and taker of notes. Toby and I usually forgot 50% of the content in shock and would have to ring up the specialist nurse afterwards to reinform ourselves.

- Be kind to yourself. Take your time – you can ask to postpone the meeting until you've had time to get over shock.

- Ask for a second opinion from another specialist doctor.
  Your doctor can and will refer you.

- You can also contact the Patient Advice and Liaison Service
  (PALS; PASS in Scotland) or the clinical ethics committee
  (CEC) at your hospital. The hospital chaplaincy can
  also help. Alternative Dispute Resolution and Mediation
  Services (ADR) are also available with further advice
  from the Children and Family Court Advisory Service
  (CAFCASS). In the US, contact the Patient Advocate
  Foundation (PAF) (see Resources).

- Look deep into yourself and be as honest as possible
  about your own motives, so you can be satisfied you're
  making decisions truly in your child's best interest. When
  you want to lose your temper, count to ten and make
  yourself say something nice to the medical team/your
  husband/your wife, because otherwise you won't be able
  to unsay it afterwards. (I think you can tell I'm speaking
  from experience!)

The most difficult thing for the doctors (aside from the very
rare disagreements with parents or a child about treatment) – I
learned this in conversation with a paediatric palliative consultant
recently – was trying to support parents who had been told
their child's death was imminent and then the child did not die.
Indeed, the child might go on to live significantly longer. The
parents had prepared themselves and were expecting it and then
can struggle with the mental torture of wondering why they
weren't necessarily as happy as they thought they should be that
their child is still alive and feeling guilty, especially if their child
had been struggling for a long time. The issue is thinking that
the prognosis (when your child is going to die) is more accurate
than it really is and not allowing for enough uncertainty. Even
in the last few hours, there is still uncertainty as to exactly when
someone will die. Trying to identify hope going forward amidst
such uncertainty and the emotional turmoil is so very hard.

Theresa's feelings when this happened to them after 'we had to make the decision to extubate him in 2011 instead of putting him through surgery' are slightly different:

> We didn't feel guilty about him not dying – I didn't anyway. Relieved for sure. The only thing I think that experience did to us was to expect that EVERY time he would miraculously be saved. It made us less aware of the signs as his actual death became closer. (See Chapter 5.)

The major medical advances of the last century seem to have come at the price of considerable psychological complexity for families. Do ask for help if this happens to you – you may have a psychologist attached to your team who can help.

TELLING THE CHILD AND THEIR SIBLINGS

This is one of the most difficult things for parents and doctors to have to do. There's no one way to approach this, although all expert advice I've ever come across, both spoken and written, agrees that, as a general rule, honesty is the best principle. Some people don't tell the child and/or the sibling/s they are going to die, and if they're little and never ask, I understand why you wouldn't. However, Alison told me that even though Ryan was only six, she wouldn't have felt right letting him go without having told him, despite it being just about the hardest thing she ever had to do. She took the opportunity one day to say there might come a time when you don't see Mummy and Daddy anymore 'but you'll always be in our hearts'.

It would be a mistake to assume that all children and young people do not want to know, that they won't understand and being told makes it worse for them. There's good evidence this is not the case and not just from the countless bucket lists shared and vlogged and blogged by young people nearing the end of their lives. I even saw a bucket list mentioned online recently from a six-year-old. This also applies equally to the siblings of the sick child or young person. Recent research conducted at the Children and

Families Research (CFR) team at Coventry University has for the first time focussed on the long-term wellbeing of bereaved adults of brothers or sisters diagnosed with life-limiting conditions. The young people 'reflected on the benefit of being included in conversations with their parents and professionals *from the time of diagnosis*, bereavement and beyond' (author's emphasis).[12]

YOUNG PEOPLE ARE THE EXPERTS IN THEIR OWN CONDITION – TIPS FOR DOCTORS (AND PARENTS!)

It is clear that young people are the experts in their own condition and will know exactly how it affects them – the key is for parents and doctors to really listen to them and not allow our own preconceptions to guide decisions on their behalf. Here are seven top tips for doctors from a group of young patients aged 11–16 at Blackpool Victoria Hospital recently[13] for talking to them. I would argue that these vital tips are even more important for their end-of-life care and they apply just as much to me as DD's mum and not just to his health professionals!

- Always check if it's okay to come in.

- Don't lie – tell me if it might hurt or things might take a while.

- It's hard for me to ask questions sometimes – please check with me if I have any.

---

12 Brown, E., Coad, J. and Franklin, A. (2017) 'The impact of a sibling's life-limiting genetic condition on adult brothers and sisters.' *American Journal of Medical Genetics Part A 173*, 7, 1754–1762.

13 Victoria's Voice Youth Forum. Victoria's Voice is the patient experience feedback for children and young people at Blackpool Victoria Hospital. It meets monthly and the views of the young people are recorded and shared. The Top Tips cards (www.bfwh.nhs.uk/childrens/docs/leaflets/Doctors%20Top%20Tips%20for%20speaking%20with%20young%20people.pdf) were developed by Victoria's Voice youth forum in October 2013, and are still used at Blackpool Hospital. The cards are primarily given to doctors and nurses in training sessions facilitated by young patients from Victoria's Voice. For HCPs wanting resources and tips for talking to young people, see www.mefirst.org.uk.

- I like to know the reasons for things – it helps me to understand.

- Encourage me to speak for myself.

- Offer me the chance to speak without my parents in the room with a chaperone.

- If you have to pass on information, please tell me.

As I'm not a psychologist, if you want detailed professional guidance in talking to your sick child or their siblings, I'm going to refer you to the recent and excellent leaflet written by professionals and parents at Children's Cancer and Leukaemia Group (CCLG). It covers children's ideas about death and how to broach the subject.[14] Together for Short Lives also has a booklet with key points.[15]

HOW IT WORKED FOR US AND OTHERS

As I've mentioned already, DD had been at the point of death several times since his diagnosis in 2007: at the beginning when they diagnosed a brain tumour; post-operative meningitis; undiagnosed hydrocephalus; and during his stem cell transplant (although that was very much under the doctor's control!). We'd got away with it, but, of course, during those times it was not our doctors' expectation that he would die, so it was never mentioned. If I'm honest, it was always what I was worried about but usually too scared to voice. Except I do remember at the very beginning pushing our brain surgeon to say what the mortality rate was for the huge operation they were about to perform. I realise now, with the benefit of hindsight and a lot more experience, that he had probably not mentioned it because he knew that it was very

---

14 CCLG (2015) *Facing the Death of Your Child: Suggestions and Help for Families, Before and Afterwards* (see Resources for details).

15 Together for Short Lives, *Difficult Conversations for Young Adults*. Free to download at www. togetherforshortlives.org.uk/professionals/resources/7837_difficult_conversations_ for_young_adults.

unlikely given that the surgery was scheduled – it was not *emergency* brain surgery. My husband and I, of course, were ignorant and just assumed all brain surgery must be equally dangerous and likely to cause our precious child's death. It is very different when you have to look death in the eye and know it's definitely coming, as we did when he relapsed the last time.

On that awful Monday in May 2012, after the MRI scan, we were ushered into a room by DD's oncologist, but his brain surgeon was also there alongside a senior nurse (an epilepsy specialist we knew well who happened to be on shift). As I say, we knew we were in big trouble but we were not sure what kind. Our oncologist then asked if we wanted DD to be there, at which point, having frozen from the inside out, I nodded. We had always told DD the truth, so that he understood why he was having to endure such horrendous treatments and trusted us. You think you can shield and protect your child by not telling them or saying that an injection won't hurt because it's what you want to believe, but I had seen at first hand that can result in the child losing trust, because injections do hurt and they know something's going on. Tragically, in some cases, they then refuse to continue treatments that might save their life because they've lost trust in *all* the adults. This decision on whether to have the child or young person present is obviously totally personal. My only comment is that over the years I kept finding that my child and the verbal children around me on the ward, of various different ages, seemed to be a lot braver at facing things than the adults (i.e. me). I discovered I had to *listen* very hard to them because I realised they were telling me what they needed but I didn't want to hear it – another 'Follow the Child' moment!

The oncologist and surgeon sat opposite Toby, DD and me, and the conversation went something like this:

Oncologist: The scans are not what we were all hoping to see.

Me: So it's not the shunt? God, I was praying for shunt surgery! [Stressed laugh]

Oncologist: No, I'm afraid not. The cancer is back. [Shocked silence]

Brain surgeon: Would you like to the see the scans?

[Pause. I absolutely didn't *like* to but knew that I wouldn't believe it unless I could see it, as I had done at his diagnosis five years before.]

Me and Toby: Okay. [We all trooped out to the nurses' station where there was a computer. The surgeon called up the images.]

Me: Where is it? [I was expecting one huge tumour like the first time.]

Surgeon: [Taking a biro from the desk, he pointed.] Here and here and here and here.

[He was pointing at dozens of little dots absolutely all over DD's brain and down his spine. Silence from all parties. We all went back into the little room. I was numb and my chest hurt so badly; if I hadn't known what it was, I'd have asked for a scan myself. Tears were streaming down my face. The nurse handed me a box of tissues. I couldn't look at my husband or child.]

Oncologist: I think it is now clear that there is no longer any chance of curing this cancer. I'm so sorry, David.

DD: So I'm going to die? [He looked towards me. I nodded in reply. Thunderous silence.]

Me to oncologist: There's nothing available anywhere in the world you would put one of your children through in this situation? [I knew he had several. I felt mean framing the question in such a way.]

Oncologist: Nothing, anywhere, at any price.

DD: Great. [Very sarcastic]

Oncologist: There are still things we can do. We could talk about chemotherapy...

[I knew he meant palliative, non-curative chemotherapy; you need to be sure in this situation, so if you're not, ask. DD had already done over two years' worth of curative and I knew it meant side-effects, blood tests, scan stress, results and check-ups. He'd had enough. We'd all had enough of that kind of intervention.]

Me: We're going home.

[Everyone looked startled and our oncologist looked at DD and then at me with a puzzled expression. Normally, DD always led the discussions but I knew something that no one in the room knew, which meant it would have been unfair to make DD responsible for his health decisions now: he had the beginnings of dementia. I knew he could no longer process things in the same way – his loss of memory was the biggest sign, but he was also slightly opaque. I don't know how else to describe it. Our oncologist looked at me; he knew me really well after nearly five years and he understood that I knew something. He nodded.]

Oncologist: [Still wrong-footed by my statement] Erm, you can go home and come back again to talk about all this later this week when you've had a chance to think, if you like?

Me: No. I think we've done quite enough hospital! We can just have complete symptoms' management at home, can't we? Can Jane come and talk to us at home? [The paediatric palliative specialist nurse, not her real name.]

Oncologist: Absolutely. We can go and book it into the diary now.

DD: No steroids. I hate them.

Me: I promise only pills that take away symptoms like headache and sickness. We're going to go home and party, my darling.

That was the meeting in essence from my point of view. Of course, it was much longer and more people spoke, including my loving husband, and they might each recall it very differently. We had had to redefine our hope from one that would mean eventual cure to hoping for a fantastic party and experiences in the short time left for and with DD. Looking back, I realise how much trust had been built up by now between the medical team and our family – we knew each other more than well by this point – a relationship akin, I imagine, to men in the trenches during the Great War (if that doesn't sound too melodramatic).

I knew we had very little time left with DD because at his initial diagnosis five years before we'd been told that from the beginning of symptoms to death was roughly six weeks if you do not treat his type of cancer. Now we had chosen maximum *quality of life* over *quantity* because I did not want to give pain, inevitable with the spinal tumours, the chance to get to the point where it can only be controlled by rendering the patient unconscious – where's the quality of life in that? That's the essence in drawing the line: weighing up whether the quantity of life potentially gained is worth it, given the direct impact of an intervention/treatment or side-effects on the quality of life left for your child. Quality of life depends on what your child loves to do. Clearly the wide range of different cancers and conditions that affect children will give a different experience at the end of life.

It is important I say that I knew the choices here in front of my child without being told by DD's medical team because I had helped my mum at home, with my siblings, when my father died of cancer. So I knew we could be at home, and my father had refused to take any medicines that would in any way prolong his life because he deemed the quality he would gain was not worth the pain, so I understood some of those discussions. Having met so many families in hospital and since campaigning, I know this is unusual. Modern medicine is so successful and death has become so medicalised and centred on hospitals, particularly in the US, that most people have no experience or knowledge of the dying process. My mum had always been really upfront with us as children about everything embarrassing – sex, death, divorce – to the extent that sometimes we wouldn't ask because we knew we'd get *too much* information! She had talked openly in the years since Dad died about not resuscitating her if she had a heart attack in old age, and then we'd all argue about exactly how old she meant! She was talked out of having DNR (Do Not Resuscitate) tattooed on to her chest after she met a paramedic who said they'd still perform it if she keeled over in the street, in case they were the initials of the love in her life! Derek Norbert Radford…how we teased her!

Theresa and Asher

Other people's experiences vary widely. Theresa's son, Asher, had Dandy-Walker malformation/syndrome, cerebral palsy, seizures and a wide range of other musculoskeletal and congenital abnormalities, diagnosed at birth, requiring intensive support and frequent hospitalisation in the PICU.

No one mentioned palliative care, not one of Theresa's providers – frankly because it does not exist in her community – or that his condition was life-limiting. No one thought to have the difficult conversation with the family 'until it was crunch time'[16] and by this time he was ten years old. Theresa writes this in capitals: TEN YEARS OLD. This is the opposite of parallel planning! Only then did they look at the world from her son's perspective – or, as she writes, from 'a truly selfless perspective' – and what is important to him, and then make decisions. Theresa and her family had 24 hours at this point in 2011 to

---

16 Article in the newsletter of the American Academy of Pediatrics, Fall 2016, Section on Bioethics: 'Just an expression', edited by Dalia Feltman, MD, p.16.

decide whether to transport Asher to a hospital six hours away to undergo a life-saving tracheostomy and laryngectomy that would mean he would be on a ventilator for the rest of his life... or let him die. Theresa refers to this conversation as their first Do Not Resuscitate (DNR) conversation (see also Chapter 2) and she recalls it as 'very awkward':

> Us: Well, what does that mean, really?
>
> MD [doctor]: Well, it can mean anything you want, really.
>
> Us: Like what?
>
> MD: [Lists an entire gamut of possible interventions that we could pick and choose from, like a death menu.]

This surgical intervention would, however, rob him of all those things that brought him joy: horseback riding, going to the beach, just basically *living*. With their loving team, the family decide against the surgical intervention. Funnily enough, that seems to be the life-saving decision and he lives another two years *without the intervention*. We will revisit Theresa again making more decisions about life-sustaining treatments in the next chapter.

Michelle and Keir

> When Keir was two, his nursery workers told us they were worried about his walking... Anyway, to cut a very long story very short and after numerous appointments with various doctors, Keir was diagnosed with a neuromuscular condition called Charcot Marie Tooth disease (CMT). This was very slowly degenerative but at worst would make him very fatigued, there was definitely no mention of it being in any way life-limiting...
>
> However, when he stared primary school, he began to deteriorate quite rapidly. He became very unsteady on his feet and had episodes of incontinence which was strange as he had been dry since the age of two.

I emailed his neurologist with these symptoms and she organised an emergency MRI scan and some blood and urine tests as these symptoms were not the norm for CMT. We went to Pendlebury Children's Hospital in Manchester for the tests and I remember asking what they were looking for. Metabolic diseases, she said. Oh that's okay, I thought, if it's something like that we can sort it out with diet or medication. Little I knew at the time. I began to Google furiously, big mistake! I had an A4 note pad on which I wrote the possible conditions that it could be – none of them good. In my heart, I think I knew then that we would lose him…

On the day, having dropped both children off at school, my husband and I drove to the hospital, parked the car and went into a building, I can't even remember the name of it but I do recall that there were people playing football on the grass outside the window. The incongruousness of this strikes me even to this day. This is how the conversation went:

> Neurologist: Keir has a condition called metachromatic leukodystrophy. You've probably never heard of it.
>
> Me: Actually I have, I've been Googling.
>
> Neurologist: It's a metabolic disease which will slowly rob him of all his previously acquired skills.
>
> Me: He's going to die, isn't he, earlier than us?
>
> Neurologist: Yes.
>
> Martin: How much earlier?
>
> Neurologist: He may not make it into double figures. He will slowly lose his skills and may lose his sight and hearing eventually.
>
> Me: Will he still know who we are?
>
> Neurologist: Yes he will know.

When she told us, I burst into tears. Not because I wanted to cry but because I thought that it was the 'expected reaction' to being told that your child may only have a few more years to live. I didn't really want to cry and in some ways I felt like a fake. I just felt numb, like someone had emptied all of my insides and filled me with cotton wool (like your mouth feels when you've had an anaesthetic at the dentist). That's how I still feel to a certain extent, though it's arguable whether it's better to continue the numbness because at least then you don't have to feel.

And the people carried on their football game. And they were laughing and living.

The drive home was and remains a complete blur. How we got home I still don't know to this day. It gives a whole new meaning to the phrase 'autopilot'. We picked Erin up from our friend's house and she asked, 'How did it go?' Martin just shook his head; neither of us could speak the words. We all went to school to collect Keir and we bought fish and chips for tea. We videoed him that evening, this beautiful blonde-haired angel, eating his tea, talking and laughing like any other five-year-old. We were broken.

Michelle and her husband were clearly told that this disease would kill their child; lack of clarity was not the problem. The problem was getting the right people, services and equipment needed, and Michelle had to fight for them tooth and nail, which I find outrageous when local authorities have a legal obligation to provide this care. Michelle had experience working for social services, but even for her trying to navigate the complexities of multiple professionals across this and the NHS was daunting. Eventually, they were referred to an amazing paediatrician and community nurse (CN) and physiotherapist who became their 'go to' people all the way through Keir's illness.

However, although they had been referred to the hospice, they didn't actually use their services until 2007 (a good two years after Keir's diagnosis). Hospice key workers can coordinate the care between all the multiple different doctors, health professionals and social care, and hugely reduce stress for families. Michelle says misunderstanding what hospices were, and palliative care generally, was what delayed their access. She too thought that 'it meant Keir was dying'. They were referred quite early on to their hospice but 'I imagined a hospital ward-type scenario with lots of bald children (because I equated hospice with cancer). When we eventually went, of course, it was nothing like that... Being able to stay meant I could have a break from the physical care (though I still fussed him) and just be his mum. Precious times indeed.'

Alison and Ryan

Alison and her husband are the only family I've met where they *did* have a palliative specialist present at their devastating diagnosis meeting. A specialist nurse from the children's community nurses responsible for palliative care was present. The meeting had been fast-tracked by their doctor and was led by a consultant paediatrician at an outpatient's clinic.

Ryan had been born a normal, healthy baby just three years before and the diagnosis of a rare, degenerative, genetic, neurological, life-threatening condition for which there was no cure and a life-expectancy of just 12 months was a total bombshell, as at that point it was not obvious. Ryan's little brother Rhys was a newborn at this point, and this meant genetic testing for him as well (fortunately, this showed he will not develop the condition). The palliative specialist nurse present at the meeting immediately linked the family to the services available in their local area. Alison recalls that she had no idea what 'palliative' meant and was initially horrified at the mention of hospice care, but in retrospect she realises it was the best thing that could have happened. At one of their regular short-break respite visits at the hospice, she was introduced to the counselling team; she explained that this meant 'they moved with the journey with you', which she sees as critical to the support her whole family received before and since Ryan's death.

Alison has sat on many palliative steering groups since Ryan died and, having witnessed the experience of many families, is adamant that this palliative input must start at the hospital at the beginning, as it did for them.

Jane and Callum

Jane and her partner were given a prognosis just six days after their second child, Callum, was born. He was without oxygen for 17 long minutes at birth. Clarity was not the problem at their Difficult Conversation; instead, it was brutality. A top paediatric neurologist flatly stated:

> He won't talk; he won't walk; he won't hold his head up; he'll have a mental age of around two years old and if he doesn't resolve his feeding issues he'll be dead in three to five years.

Jane told me this conversation could easily have been improved with the magic ingredient of hope. Her father went to speak to that neurologist's registrar afterwards, and although the doctor confirmed that these were the outcomes for a lot of children they had worked with like Callum, he went on to say positively that 'you get out what you put in'. In other words, engaging with services and adhering to therapy regimes would make such a short life expectancy less likely. He was right, and Callum, with his family's dedicated care, lived to just short of his ninth birthday.

Jane's introduction to palliative care was not for a couple of years:

> Even then, the idea that a child's palliative care journey could take years wasn't one explained to me. The formal palliative care team didn't get involved though until Callum had spent a month in absolute agony, some of it over the Christmas period in 2010.

By this time he was five years old and this was at one of the UK's most prestigious children's hospitals. Hearing this made me understand the depth of her passion for improving palliative and end-of-life care.

REACTIONS OF MEMBERS OF THE FAMILY TO THE DIFFICULT CONVERSATION – SIBLINGS AND PARENTS

DD's developing dementia meant there was a delay this time in his reaction. At his first cancer relapse, aged 13, in 2009, he had immediately said in the car on the way home: 'Did you know the Chinese have the same word for crisis and opportunity?' I did not know and frankly at that point was trying to drive in torrential rain and rush-hour traffic and wished the Chinese could sit in my seat at that moment! He went on to say: 'Well, I'd better carry on going to school and doing my exams because I'm going to look a bit stupid if after all this I survive!' (He was going to have to do a ton more treatment to have a chance of cure.) So we'd agreed that we would focus all our energy on confining his timetable (and his whole life) just to the things that would get him to his dream of going to university and reading one of the sciences. All he said after that was: 'You and Dad will be okay? You'll carry on doing your usual stuff?' This was what he was worrying about. I swore we would.

This time, in 2012, we got home, shocked and overwhelmed. (The car journey invariably would have been a 'safe' conversation about what we all wanted to eat for supper, and DD always had very strong ideas on that subject.) Toby let our support network know by ringing my sister, the information hub for our community, who sent out a mass email to make sure everyone knew what was going on. DD, meanwhile, had gone to his room. I was cooking dinner and he came down and logged on to his Facebook page on the computer in the kitchen. Minutes later we had the following conversation:

DD: Mum, I've told my friends that I've had it and I'm going to die and they all say I've got to carry on fighting. [He was visibly distressed.]

Me: That's all they ever hear in the wretched newspapers and they don't understand. Okay. Tell them that chemotherapy does cure a lot of cancer but if it hasn't worked, it gets to the point where, having any more gives you more cancer. Then ask them if they'll all come to a big party here. We'll figure out a date tomorrow when we're less tired.

This worked and everyone said they'd be there. Rufus and Holly by this time had been told that their brother's cancer cannot be cured and it would kill him, probably quite soon. They said very little. They were used to trying to process very difficult information. I'll quote two sisters here speaking about their experience with a sibling who lives and then dies from Sanfilippo syndrome:[17]

One thing you do have to do is grow up and make your own decisions much quicker than other children may have to…we had to be more independent.

I definitely recognise this in Rufus and Holly. I asked if there's anything they wanted to know. They shook their heads, so we settled on a movie and pizza; life continued.

Later that night DD came into our room just as we were about to turn the lights off. He cut to the chase (that's children and young people all over!):

'If I'm going to die soon and Gary [his doctor] can't do anything, why can't I just take a pill now and get it over with?'

This was not a conversation that could be postponed to the morning and I knew that would be exactly what I would think

---

17 *Lives Worth Living: Fifteen Stories of Exceptional Children Whose Short Lives Left a Lasting Legacy*, p.106.

if I was facing my own death, and it's certainly what my late father had wanted to do. I didn't want to get bogged down in the fact that the Assisted Suicide Bill was at that very moment in time trudging its way through the legal process in the House of Lords. The real point was that I understood DD was frightened about the *process* of getting to death, not about death as an idea (his interest in Buddhism had put paid to that).

> Me: Do you remember the last time you were nearly dead?

> DD: No. [DD looked interested albeit slightly shocked.]

> Me: Right. Just like all those times, you won't know. We'll have all the medicines to keep you comfortable and until then we can party and have fun. How does that sound?

> DD: Good.

This was clearly what he wanted to know, so he said goodnight and left. I had to take half a lorazepam, as I knew my levels of distress were such that I would not sleep. I was prescribed this amount by a brilliant paediatrician during one of DD's hospital stays. Cleverly, he had identified why I had, up to this point, not done anything about my extreme sleep deprivation: I thought I would not be able to awaken if DD needed me. The doctor told me this amount meant I would get to sleep but would be able to wake up and deal with DD but then be able to go back to sleep. It was what he himself took for jetlag. That convinced me. This care saved my life. (I tried not to take more than two doses in a week as they're addictive.) Without sleep, it takes me three days before I start to unravel via unpredictable panic attacks, loss of the feeling that I can cope and appetite loss, and I know I'm unsafe. I'm horrified when I look back at the times I was driving and I should not have been, but you get to the point where your decision making is so impaired that choice is impossible, so you're on a dodgy autopilot. Any health professional reading this, please make sure you watch out for these signs in your families.

Michelle and Keir

Michelle's daughter was around the same age as Holly when she had to process that her little brother had a life-shortening condition. I'll leave Michelle to explain what happened:

> Erin was and still is very emotionally tuned in and we thought she would be able to process the enormity of this news, albeit in her seven-year-old brain. Plus, we were absolutely broken and you can't hide that, no matter how hard you try (although, as the years tick by, your acting skills would win you an Oscar). So we told her. She asked some questions, though I can't recollect exactly what, but I remember us trying to answer them as honestly as possible. That foundation we laid was one of the best decisions we made throughout the whole of Keir's illness. She was able to make her own decisions about how she wanted to spend time with her brother and what memories she wanted to make, though this was tested to the limit when he bit her on the lip as she tried to give him a kiss one night. (Biting was one of the strange behaviours he developed as the white matter in his brain slowly started to unravel. There were others, all of them fleeting but each one marked a further deterioration.)
>
> Siblings are often forgotten in the process of grief, but their loss is as great as a parent's. They will suddenly go from carefree child to dealing with emotions that most adults would struggle to deal with.[18]

Theresa and Asher

> Asher is the youngest of four. His oldest brother, Alex, is nine years older, Andrew is five years older, and Maddi is three years older. Although he had significant physical and cognitive delays (he couldn't speak, walk, or purposefully use his hands), he was treated like 'one of the gang' and his condition was just accepted. As the children grew older, they learned how to care

---

18 From *Keir's Story*, Together for Short Lives newsletter, issue 11, December 2014, p.6.

for him as much as they learned how to incorporate him into their play: changing his diaper; administering his medications; feeding him through his g-tube; reading to him; sitting him between them while playing video games or just 'hanging out' at the mall (he was, after all, a 'chick magnet'!). They were also used to frequent doctor appointments and hospitalizations so his dying was sort of an unspoken reality in our house. I think the kids were more acutely aware, or at least could see the proverbial writing on the wall, whilst my husband, David, and I were in denial: I recall being asked numerous times by friends and even medical providers, 'When are you all going to go on a Make-A-Wish trip?' and responding with, 'Why we would we take him on a Make-A-Wish trip? Those are for kids who are going to die?' Yes, I actually said that.

Even though he didn't communicate verbally, Asher was usually full of life and joy. His smile and laugh were infectious. When it was clear that Asher was actively dying, and we had to make the decision to move from attempts to make him better to ensuring he wasn't hurting, we talked with all of the kids. As hard as it was, they knew he was ready to go. My children demonstrated their selfless love for their brother.

Chapter 2

THE DIFFICULT CONVERSATION PART II

THE ADVANCE CARE PLAN

'Planning ahead doesn't mean giving up; you never give up, you always have hope; you never stop chasing rainbows...'

Kimberley[1]

Everyone is apprehensive about having to think and talk about death before it happens. So perhaps it's useful to compare planning before a birth. You would not dream of having a baby without speaking to another mother about what it was like or reading a book or two or going to antenatal classes. You are taught what to expect and what to look out for medically – what the symptoms are of pre-eclampsia, who to call and what to do. You also record your wishes as to the type of birth you would like to achieve – your birth plan. We do not discriminate about who is given this information either – it's for everyone regardless of background, gender, religion, nationality, education, disability or financial circumstances. When your child is facing the end of life and is going to die, we are effectively midwives for them leaving the world and, like these professionals, we need similar skills and information to enable that to happen in as calm and comfortable a way as possible – a death plan. There is no rehearsal for either

---

1   *Lives Worth Living: Fifteen Stories of Exceptional Children Whose Short Lives Left a Lasting Legacy*, p.94.

birth or death – only one chance to get it right – so planning and good communication between everyone involved is vital.

I would never say I was in total control of DD's death, any more than I had been for his birth, but having the information I needed and having acquired nursing skills along the way, and getting the nurses to supply any I lacked, meant I was empowered to manage this at home. I knew this was what DD wanted. The core of the information I needed was in drawing up the advance care plan (ACP), although I didn't know this was what it was called until long after DD died. I would have liked to have known this, have been given that formal introduction by our nurse, as plans reassure me. It was having the what-if conversations: if we have another emergency and this time treatment doesn't work, what would we want to happen?

If you'd like to listen to parents who have done this planning, there's a beautiful, short, film testimony called 'Jack's Story'.[2] Note that the parents had very early palliative support and I particularly liked the father saying it helped them 'see the future' for Jack instead of limitation.

> First off, there are no rules about this; an ACP is *not* legally binding in the UK and you can change your mind right up to the last second (just as with a birth plan). In the US, it is legally binding but can be revoked at any time.

WHAT IS IT?

It is a document that records in advance all the choices and wishes the young person/child and family have for the end of life *in their own words* in order that everyone caring for them knows what is most important to them and this will guide all decisions. It shouldn't just be medical choices but also practical, spiritual and emotional ones. A brief statement on

---

2   'Anticipatory Care Planning: Jack's Story', vimeo.com/203791630.

age-appropriate understanding, educational ability and how your child communicates is also best practice. If your child has a long palliative care history, you may already have drawn up a child-centred planning document. This ACP is just an extension of that.[3]

There is no generic form of ACP as different areas in the UK are developing their own based on an NHS template.[4] A copy is held by *all* the health care professionals (HCPs) who care for your family in any capacity and related professionals who may be responsible for your child such as teachers at school. DD would have been at school in those last three months, but his friends were sitting their GCSEs and classes had ceased. The clever thing now is that once you've drawn up your ACP, secure digital copies can be shared, with your/the family's permission, between all the services so that there is less chance of communication failure in an emergency. Crucially, this all means you don't have to endlessly explain the history, medication, wishes and whose care you/your child are under and where to different health professionals, which is so exhausting.[5]

In the US, Theresa's paediatrician in Florida uses a DNR document (see below) instead of an ACP as there are no specialist children's palliative services there. Eventually, via the Assistant Professor of Pediatrics at the University of California, San Francisco (UCSF), I found the one they use there: Voicing My Choices: A Planning Guide for Adolescents and Young Adults.[6] This ACP was developed by researchers at the Pediatric

---

3   In the UK, if you already have a Wiki platform as part of your/your child's personal care plan, you can just add your ACP to be shared with all your health professionals.

4   See www.cypacp.nhs.uk. See also template ACP for the West Midlands Paediatric Palliative Care Network: www.togetherforshortlives.org.uk/assets/0000/1486/6c_Advance_Care_Plan_2012.pdf. In Wales they have called it the PAC-plan (Paediatric Advance Care plan): http://wales.pallcare.info; for Scotland, see www.cen.scot.nhs.uk/palliative-care.

5   The NHS is trialling a system in London called Coordinate My Care (http://coordinatemycare.co.uk); a patient portal allows you to see it and any updates/changes made are automatically recorded. Outside London, #KnowAboutMe is being rolled out by NHS England and National Council for Palliative Care (NCPC).

6   https://agingwithdignity.org/shop/product-details/voicing-my-choices. You have to pay to download this; it is available in English and Spanish.

Oncology Branch, National Cancer Institute and the National Institutes of Mental Health at the National Institutes of Health, and included extensive research using the Five Wishes advance directive[7] and incorporating the feedback of adolescents and young adults. A mature eight- or nine-year-old can do it but it is typically used for children aged 13 years and older. For parents of younger children, the 'My Wishes' document is used as a guide for using open-ended questions to get at what the parents understand about their child's illness, their needs, how the child is feeling, their experience with illness and how they/ their family maintain their strength.

WHO DRAWS IT UP?

It is drawn up by the family and child, if they wish to, with the whole medical and support team or just one nominated representative of it who can liaise and advocate for/with the family. It could be a paediatric palliative specialist nurse, if there is one, or another nurse with whom you all have a good relationship or your hospice key worker, or someone in the learning disability services who may already have helped with child-centred planning. It's utterly flexible, and if it can be someone whom you already know and trust, clearly that will make an incredibly painful conversation just that little easier to bear.

Should your child lack the mental capacity to make particular decisions for themselves and they are approaching adulthood and their shift towards legal status as decision makers, Together for Short Lives has a range of resources providing useful information.[8]

---

7   The website of National Healthcare Decisions Day (www.nhdd.org/public-resources/#where-can-i-get-an-advance-directive) has lots of brilliant contacts and information including this link: www.aha.org/advocacy-issues/initiatives/piiw/state. shtml which gives state links.

8   See their factsheet on the Mental Capacity Act 2005 (MCA) (www.togetherforshortlives. org.uk/families/information_for_families/4980_the_mental_capacity_act). See also My Adult – Still My Child (http://myadultstillmychild.co.uk).

WHERE DOES IT GET DRAWN UP?

Anywhere you feel comfortable! At home, or at a hospice you're already linked to – anywhere.

WHEN DOES IT GET DRAWN UP?

It's part of the series of difficult conversations that hopefully get you to the point where you feel as ready to cope as you'll ever be. There's no set pattern for when this is done – we did ours the week after DD's incurable diagnosis because time was short. If your child has regular check-ups with someone in your team, it could be at any one of those. Once it's done, the good thing then is that you know it's filed with all the professionals who need to know and you/your family can just get on with living. You don't have to discuss it ever again until you're actually in the moment or something changes and you want to update the plan to reflect this. Alison puts it best: 'We got our pegs in place and moved them accordingly.'

WHAT TO DO BEFORE THE MEETING – HOW DO I APPROACH IT?

This is the core of your planning. I know I needed to summon up the courage to name, say out loud, what I was worried about; if I hadn't, it would have festered and added to the cocktail of stress.

> Cocktail = fear + sleeplessness + oestrogen + progesterone + testosterone + adrenaline (fight/flight) + cortisol (stress hormone) + grief+ love

Before the meeting (do this every time you revisit your ACP as things change):

- Write your worries down (the stress cocktail made me very forgetful), so you can make sure your health professional can address them one by one.

Becca Riley, an experienced palliative care nurse and Clinical Associate with Gold Standards Framework, has helped many children and families with this process and trains health professionals and families. She encourages the use of person-centred thinking and planning to help children, young people and family/carers think about and discuss the challenges they face and the choices they wish to make regarding their end-of-life care. It helps identify when the balance of life-prolonging treatments versus pure symptom management for comfort has changed. These person-centred planning approaches include thinking about and writing down:

  – What is important to me (my child) to ensure I am (they are) happy and fulfilled and what is important for me (my child) to ensure I am (they are) safe and healthy?

  – What's working; what's not working in my (your child's) care?

  – What do I (does my child) want now and in the future? My (their) hopes and fears.

  – What does a Good Day and a Bad Day look like?

  – If I (my child) could, I (my child) would...

NB. You could also draw a picture and/or make a video as your answer.

To see how Becca has used this approach to planning with families, go to her toolkit in the Appendix. (It can also be downloaded separately as a template by healthcare professionals at www.jkp.com/catalogue/book/9781785923463.)

At the meeting(s), go through the next sections with the answers in mind because it will inform your choices. Some ACPs do not have all of them, so be sure to bring them up if your health professional doesn't. You need to ensure that by the end of the meeting(s), you have an idea of what to expect as your/ child's disease progresses. This is very, very hard to hear, but without it the inevitable medical crises will be a shock and then we panic and you/your child can end up in the one place no one wanted.

WHAT TREATMENTS DO YOU WANT OR NOT WANT FOR YOUR CHILD, INCLUDING DO NOT RESUSCITATE (DNR) DECISIONS?

Once you have an understanding from your health professionals about how your child's condition tends to progress, there may be treatments or interventions (life-sustaining treatments – LSTs) that you can choose to accept or refuse, depending on how they will impact on your/their life. In the UK these are deliberately no longer called life-*saving* treatments to show that they are not going to cure your child's condition/disease – they are *prolonging* life. Decisions are always made on the basis of whether or not treatment is in the child's best interests. Obviously, there is a big range of treatments due to the huge number of diseases, with everything from aggressive, intensive intervention through to minimal. They can be for a gradual decline or a sudden emergency. Some treatments are only available in hospital in high-dependency units (HDU or NICU or PICU), which may affect your decision – for example, invasive intubation and ventilation when a tube is put down the throat and attached to mechanical breathing equipment. For us, any treatment that would have resulted in hospitalisation for DD was out of the question.

Often doctors talk in terms of either stopping (*withdrawing*) a treatment that a child is already on – for example, mechanical ventilatory (breathing) equipment – or trying to explain that they don't think it would be a good idea to start (*withholding*) a treatment they think would not work and/or would do more harm to a child from horrible side-effects than good. If you're facing these conversations in NICU/PICU, the booklet/online resource written by the Royal Children's Hospital in Melbourne,[9] has really useful lists of questions you can ask your doctors and a full list of the types of treatment. It also identifies how, emotionally, it seems easier not to start a treatment than to have to decide to stop one for your child, whilst also stating that for some people knowing that it has been tried and not worked can be helpful. If you want to understand how health professionals approach this, Together for Short Lives has a guide for them specifically on compassionate extubation – removing tubes, whether for life-sustaining breathing or food or drugs – at the end of life.[10]

A bereaved parent who knew their baby was not going to survive describes this process being well handled by their health professionals:

> Staff informed me of [the] decisions we would have to make beforehand so we weren't rushed or shocked when we had to make them.[11]

NB. If you disagree with your doctors, see section 'What you can do if you disagree' in Chapter 1.

In terms of cancer treatment, for the sake of clarity, I will repeat here that chemotherapy or radiotherapy or immunotherapy at this point are not curative; they are buying time and it depends on which cancer and your child's history and their wishes whether you and your team feel this would be in your/their best interest. I've heard families say: 'Well, surely the doctor would have said if X was going to die?' and 'X's on chemotherapy, so...' – the

---

9   Wilkinson, D., Gallam, L., Hynson, J., Sullivan and Xafis, V. (2013) *Caring Decisions*, www.rch.org.au/caringdecisions/chapters/Different_types_of_treatment.

10 See www.togetherforshortlives.org.uk/professionals/care_provision/care_pathways/extubation_care_pathway.

11 National Perinatal Epidemiology Unit, 'Listening to parents after stillbirth or the death of their baby after birth', www.npeu.ox.ac.uk/listeningtoparents, p.31.

family assumes, because the doctor has not made it clear, that the chemotherapy will cure their beloved. If you're not sure what the doctor is saying, ask! When we decided at our first Difficult Talk to have symptoms' control only for DD, I meant no interventions that might increase his life expectancy *at all*. That included refusing to put a feeding tube in when he was no longer able to eat or to ventilate him – withholding those life-sustaining treatments. We would also have refused for DD to be given antibiotics had he contracted pneumonia or indeed any type of serious infection for the same reason – it was kinder with his particular disease and history not to be given anything that would slow down his death. For DD, it was quality of life over quantity every time, but it totally depends on the disease and the child.

Do Not Resuscitate (DNR) and Do Not Attempt Cardio-Pulmonary Resuscitation (DNACPR)

Be reassured: DNR (sometimes referred to in the US as No Code) does not mean do not treat at all! If a doctor phrases this as 'withdrawing care', they do not mean *all* care, just a particular treatment that is not working. You can have many other life-sustaining treatments such as antibiotics for an infection or oxygen but choose not to resuscitate only in the specific case of cardiac arrest – of the heart stopping. This confusion must be why they now call it DNACPR so it's clear it is something specific. In the US you can sign a Physician's Orders for Life-Sustaining Treatment (POLST) for your child to make sure cardiac resuscitation (CPR) does not happen in an emergency. The language is not ideal for children/parents, but emergency services know this and therefore are careful how they talk about it. There is a really good leaflet online by POLST California.[12] However, I'm aware from Theresa that POLST has not reached Florida – they have a DNR form and very few parents currently

---

12 Children's Hospice and Paliative Care Coalition/POLST California, Using POLST with the Pediatric Population, https://med.fsu.edu/userfiles/file/POLST%20in%20 Pediatrics.pdf. For the most recent form, see http://capolst.org/2016polst.

sign them. I would humbly like to suggest a connection here between the lack of specialist children's palliative networks and parents not signing. At UCSF in San Francisco, where they do have those services, most parents do sign once they've been talked through it. There's no right or wrong way; it is deeply personal to the family and child, but honest conversations are necessary. The horrific repercussions of not doing this are shown by another US family without those services (see Chapter 5).

Given the state of DD's disease and after talking to our medical team, we signed a DNACPR form. Otherwise, had he gone into cardiac arrest at home and we had panicked and called an ambulance to the house, we might have insisted that the paramedics administer CPR even though they would be aware this would be against DD's best interest. This would have been incredibly distressing and violent to see administered; it would also have been highly unlikely to work, given that it would have been happening because he was dying from advanced cancer. Even if it had worked, the forceful chest compressions often damage the ribs and/or give brain damage, so DD would have been kept alive for a very short period of time but with an even worse quality of life. So, in that situation, it was far better for DD and for us to have decided *in advance* not to intervene and let a heart attack take his life. Callum had developed osteopaenia, so Jane Green says that 'a full resuscitation would have caused catastrophic injuries. He didn't deserve that.' Therefore, Jane had written down in their care plan exactly which treatments health professionals could administer if he stopped breathing, but she signed a DNACPR in the case of his heart stopping. Her own name for this was 'a partial DNR'.

PLACE OF DEATH (PoD)

This is sometimes now referred to as place of care, but place of care and place of death are two different but related things. So there's the place you might like to be in the last months and weeks and then where you would like to be for the actual death: they don't have to be the same place.

Where do you/does your child eventually want to be? The choices are:

- in hospital

- in a hospice

- at home.

Hospital

In my experience, most people have no idea that their child does *not* have to die in hospital. Hospitals are kitted out for cure, for sterility, not dying, and whilst they can keep your child comfortable, it is very difficult for them to attend to the emotional and spiritual needs of a dying child or young person.

I find it interesting that the place in the UK with the highest proportion of hospital deaths and the lowest of home deaths for children and young people with cancer is London.[13] I imagine this is because there are plenty of hospitals within easy reach and many of London's hospitals have a worldwide reputation, often linked to their proximity to university research departments, and therefore it is assumed that this means they must be the best place to die. What most people are unaware of is that the things that need to be done medically to make you comfortable at the end of life can *all* be done at home or in a hospice. In this it differs from birth: you can't have a caesarean section at home, for example! Wessex, where I live, is the area with the reverse proportion – most deaths happening at home/hospice – and we now have good clinical networks with appropriately trained health professionals in the community to deliver that care, which means parents have a meaningful choice for PoD.

---

13 Gao, W., Verne, J., Peacock, J., Stiller, C. *et al.* (2016) 'Place of death in children and young people with cancer and implications for end of life care: A population-based study in England 1993–2014.' *BMC Cancer*, https://bmccancer.biomedcentral.com/articles/10.1186/s12885-016-2695-1.

I completely understand that for babies, given that many mothers often have warning the birth is going to be difficult and even that their baby is going to die or has already died, then you have to be in hospital for best care on the labour ward or on the neonatal intensive care unit (NICU). Also, if most of your child's care has been delivered in acute settings, you might feel more comfortable staying there, given that the staff will have become second family − a surrogate community if you will (see Theresa's story below). The situation can also arise that a child or young person cannot be moved safely home from an intensive care setting if it has been left very late; they are too fragile.

NB. If you wish to donate whole organs (see below) to save another child/young person's life, you will almost certainly need to be in hospital for the death as your child will need to be on a ventilator and the surgery needs to be carried out very quickly after death.

However, outside of those examples, here's a list of the reasons why hospital is not an ideal place for your child to die:

- Often, there are not as many nursing staff per patient as in a hospice/hospice homecare. It does depend which type of ward you are on − acute/higher dependency units, like the one Theresa and Asher were on in Florida, come with a higher staff-to-patient ratio. A paediatric palliative team in the US and UK, if one exists in your hospital, are only in the building during office hours but remain on call at night 24/7, 365 days a year.

- Technically, there's only bed space for one parent to sleep next to them on the ward (if the other parent wants a bed, they have to go into the parent/family hostel). Siblings can't be there, whereas they can at home and in a hospice. In Florida, Asher's siblings did stay if they wanted. However, just as in the UK, there was only one designated 'bed': 'David and I took turns sleeping in the bed with Asher and on the "bench bed" in the room. His sister slept on the recliner when she wanted to stay the night.'

- Unless you question whether they are necessary for your child's care, professionals will wake your child up for obs (medical observations) through the night as routine – temperature, blood pressure checks and so on – which means their quality of sleep is poor and then they can't enjoy fun things the next day as much, as they're even more tired. This is much less likely to happen in a hospice and it wouldn't happen at home. In the US, Theresa and her husband made the request and it was agreed to eliminate unnecessary temperature checks and the like. As in: 'For real, you do NOT need to know his temperature every four hours.'

- Rubber mattresses – DD hated sliding around on these. (So did I!)

- No pets – a major consideration for our family! They're family and make us happy and less stressed. In the US, there are visits from therapy pets to alleviate this, and I know in the UK you can get special permission sometimes to have your pet in hospital, but these are single visits, not permanent as at home.

- It's noisy and smells like a hospital and is therefore more stressful, especially if another child or young person is in pain or very ill close by. You can't control your physical environment with all your toys and music and smells as you can at home/hospice.

- Your friends can't stay on sleepovers – they can in a hospice or at home.

- Hospital food! Despite having become something of an expert at providing DD with home food in hospital (he refused to eat most hospital food), it was very difficult due to lack of fridge space and lack of enough cooking facilities. At home he could and did cook alongside me right up until a few days before he died. Theresa also pointed out: 'The biggest thing was the EXPENSE! Holy crap! Even if the food was decent, you can't spend four weeks eating every meal out! You know you've been there so many times for so many years when the cafeteria staff think you're a hospital employee and give you the employee discount. True story.'

- Once your child has died, it's difficult for a hospital to give you the space and time you might need, although I'm sure some manage beautifully. (This is not true for stillbirths and neonates – some units even have a dedicated room away from the post-natal ward where the father can stay and family can visit.)

- Very few hospitals have linked bereavement support from the staff you've become very close to, who understand and went through the death with you. The exceptions are if it is a stillbirth or neonatal death, in which case parents in the UK can have home visits, if they wish, from a bereavement midwife in the team for as long as they need. Great Ormond Street Hospital, Birmingham Children's Hospital, Alder Hey Children's Hospital and Bristol Royal Hospital for Children do have linked support after children and young people have died.[14] Theresa certainly had none at her hospital in the US and I didn't either.

Hospice

These are some reasons why a hospice is a good idea (on top of what I've already mentioned):

- They're not sad. Enabling play and fun and abolishing the restrictions of the child's illness as far as possible is core to what they do. As Kathy Hull, the founder of the

---

14 Generally, the bereavement team is led by the family liaison nurse, normally qualified at sister-level in PICU. You can choose to speak to someone who did 'walk with you' or only meets you after your child has died, if you prefer that separation,

first US children's hospice puts it in her Ted talk: 'The default answer is Yes and the default question, Why not?' She sees her job as providing the space to find meaning and joy at the end of life for a child, however young.

- They have lots of specialist equipment for play as well as for medical need: eye-activated computers, wheelchair trampolines, hydro-pools and sensory rooms.

- If you've recently moved and do not have lots of local friends and community to support you at home, a hospice can provide that vital support.

- There may well be much more space than at home for the family to enjoy time together and food/cleaning is all *done!* You are *all* looked after. If your children share a bedroom and moving a big bed for your sick child down to the living room can't work, I think that's a major reason to decamp to the local hospice. For split families, it provides space on neutral territory where both parents can care together but avoid clashes.

- One key worker, whom you see all the time, coordinates everything for you, making continuity of care much easier to achieve. They are your one-stop phone call, whatever stage you're at. When you're exhausted (who isn't?), that continuity is a lifeline. It's easier to relax when you know your child is with a nurse they like and you don't have to brace yourself for shift changes. It's more complicated if you've got multiple agencies coming in and out, as we did at home, however much the charities try to send the same nurses. DD's specialist paediatric palliative nurse was based an hour and a half away, at the hospital, so I only actually saw her three times on home visits, although we spoke regularly on the phone. In the UK, hospice key workers are qualified children's nurses. They then sometimes receive special tailored competency training according to the needs of specific children. They work alongside either a paediatric palliative consultant (Level 4) from the regional hospital or a paediatric consultant from the local hospital with an interest in palliative care (Level 3).

- There's often free massage available to help relieve stress.

- There's nearly always free counselling available on tap for the entire family; furthermore, this begins the moment you start to be supported by the hospice. Play and art therapy shared activities are particularly valuable for siblings who might feel uncomfortable sitting down in a one-to-one counselling session. Small bites of counselling, starting early on, then lay the foundations for dealing with the hardest process any parent has to face – the death of their child. A recent study conducted by Bournemouth University and Julia's House Hospice found that 64% of divorced or separated parents cited having a child with complex needs as a reason for the breakdown of their relationship, and, of these couples, three-quarters had no access to short breaks in a children's hospice. A parent who had had access stated: 'It saved our marriage and kept our family together.'[15]

- After your child has died, there is usually linked bereavement support from people you know at the hospice who understand what you've been through and have been counselling the whole family from the start. There is someone checking you have a hot meal and support to go back to at home.

- As part of bereavement support, many hospices offer an annual Memorial Day to celebrate the lives of the children who have died – both in the hospice and out in the community. I know my greatest fear has always been

---

15   See www.juliashouse.org for more information.

that DD would not be remembered, so this is a vital way to support families after the death.[16]

Home

The reasons why home is a good idea (on top of what I've already mentioned):

- There's no place like home!

- You don't have to decamp anywhere and all your local friends and family can pile in and help. This local, community aspect meant many friends had seen and been with us and therefore *afterwards* it helped me not isolate myself in grief. I didn't have to explain. I realise more and more that this is very important and can imagine the impossibility of a community understanding what happened to a family where the death happened over weeks/months in a hospital miles away. I particularly treasure still regularly seeing the district nurse who nursed DD at the end because her child is in the children's choir I run at our school. From this perspective, continuity of care didn't stop when DD died.

There are various options at home in terms of medical back-up in the UK:

- *Either* with community medical support led by your child's hospital medical team but delivered by your GP and its pharmacy. This team would include a district nurse or ideally a community nurse or children's nurse if they have one, with extra back-up from Macmillan support and/or Marie Curie.[17] We were very lucky that our GP's

---

16 Southampton General Hospital does organise a memorial for all the children who have died in the previous couple of years; we attended.

17 Marie Curie do not normally nurse children but they said that as DD was 16 and, crucially, 'as there is a good plan in place', they would help. Here is where my obsession with telling everyone about planning took hold – without one, they wouldn't have helped.

surgery also had the Gold Standards Framework training in end-of-life care recommended by the Royal College of General Practitioners, which meant all the planning was in place.

- *Or* with accompanying hospice care – hospice homecare – that would supplement the first option above with the crucial addition of a key worker who coordinates for the family. This service is only available in some places in the UK, but fortunately it's expanding. For hospices who offer this service to families, this is where most of their work happens. My local hospice, Julia's House, has 115 families/beds out in the community being supported this way. If we'd only been signposted to this option, this is what we would have chosen, and it's available where we live. I'm particularly aware of how helpful the linked bereavement support for us all would have been – we had nothing because the community care route does not yet supply this in the UK. Also the misinformation we received after DD's death would have been avoided as hospices know what choices are available to parents.

  In the US, this is the more common version of hospice services but this is mostly for adults; there are very few specialised services for children who have very different needs. Adult hospices accepting children are very far from ideal, as you will see in Theresa's story in Chapter 3.

- With the assistance of a death doula (UK)/death midwife (US)/soul midwife. These are often (but not always) non-medical professionals who have been trained to assist and offer comfort and support to people as they die and afterwards. You book them and pay them as you do birth doulas.[18]

---

18 In the US, I've only heard about them in New York where they are volunteers.

ANTI-PANIC PROTOCOL – EMERGENCY SCENARIOS
The ReSPECT form[19]

You may now come across this form in the UK. It is being trialled specifically to record your/your child's choices in order to guide decision-making by doctors specifically in *emergency* situations after a sudden collapse where you/your child are/is not able to make decisions or express your/their wishes. It's possible you/your child could have a sudden collapse at school when you are not there and maybe cannot be immediately reached; this form would mean your wishes are documented. It includes DNACPR decisions (see above). It should signpost to other ACP documents if not be an integral part of one, but it can be stand-alone.

How to prevent your child's admission to hospital in a sudden medical collapse

Anti-panic protocol is not an official name – it's mine. I knew I definitely wanted calm – I didn't want DD or his siblings or their visiting friends ever to be scared by what was going on – no panic. This means that you have to tell them what is likely to happen so that they are not alarmed when it does and know what to do. This links back to understanding how your child's disease is likely to progress. For example, I explained to Holly and Rufus and anyone who arrived on a visit what a seizure was likely to look like, that it was not nice to see but that it was normal for someone with DD's disease. They were instructed to fetch me straight away, as I had medicine to sort it out. Holly would say to her brother before they went to walk the dog, 'Are you going to go weird?' Once, just to wind her up, DD then mimed a seizure! (Never work with children and animals!) My reaction as a grown-up was always mortification – how could

---

19 **Re**commended **S**ummary **P**lan for **E**mergency **C**are and **T**reatment. See www.respectprocess.org.uk. This is similar to the Physician's Orders for Life-Sustaining Treatment POLST/MOLST forms in the US – see above).

his sister say something like that? But then I worked out that it meant DD was being treated as a person, a sibling first and sick cancer patient *last*, and he loved it!

If you know your child does not want to go back to hospital under any circumstances – DD didn't – you must let your health professional know and it will be recorded on the plan. Many ambulance services now have the facility to record ACP and the ReSPECT documents, and they will then be aware before they arrive. If you haven't thought about this and your child becomes unconscious, you would probably panic and call an ambulance, and if it is not recorded in writing that you do not want them to go to hospital, by law in the UK they have to be taken. For us, for DD, that would have been horrific. Having read a few blogs by paramedics, I also know it's much easier for them to respond to an emergency call to a house like ours when they know exactly what the family expects them to do. They would have been expected to support our family practically and emotionally in this scenario because, had this happened, I would have called them knowing they could have been there within about 15 minutes, whereas the GP or district nurse, typically, couldn't get there for a few hours.

How to reduce the chance of an unexpected death[20]

Having this type of good communication between services can also reduce the chance of a death at home being ruled 'unexpected', which would often result in the speed response of the police being called to verify that the death is not suspicious and potentially the body being taken by the ambulance service to the hospital mortuary as the property of the coroner.

If you're at home in the UK, you can ask your GP for a Statement of Intent (SOI). This states that a death is expected within a fortnight and is revisited every two weeks to keep it

---

20   See 'unexpected death' in Chapter 5.

up to date. Ask what is in place out of hours or at weekends, so that if your GP is unavailable or on holiday or moving surgeries (yes, this does happen, according to Michelle who worked in a coroner's office) when your child dies, he/she has nominated someone else to be in place to take the call and be able to issue the MCCD (Medical Certification of Cause of Death – see 'Certification of death' in Chapter 5). Michelle had this really well covered with Keir (see 'Keir and Michelle' in Chapter 5).

You can also ask your medical team if it would be helpful to contact the local coroner in advance to warn them that your child's death is imminent. The situation is complicated in the UK as arrangements vary according to the individual coroner. This means in some places all deaths are reported to the coroner whether they are expected or not, and the police are asked to attend if the coroner is not available. At least if you know this, it would then not be a shock.

In the US, each state has different laws, so if you are going home with your child, ask your hospice agency or palliative care team to plan ahead for you and check with your local state's coroner's office in order to minimise the number of professionals called to attend after your child's death and so that you know what to expect.

THE WISHES – MAKING MEMORIES AND RECORDING THEM

I have read some wonderful statements by young people of all ages when they are given the opportunity to fulfil their wishes.[21] This means I find it very distressing when doctors contact me on Twitter and say that a young person has asked them to ask their parents to let them make plans for their death, but the parents won't. I should say the parents *can't*, in the sense that you need a massive amount of support to be able to face this, and if you're

---

21   Again, see Stephen Sutton, *Contact Magazine*, Issue 64, Autumn 2014, Children's Cancer and Leukaemia Group (CCLG), www.cclg.org.uk/write/MediaUploads/Contact%20magazine/1%20Magazine%20pdfs/Contact_64.pdf.

not given it, if you're not linked to people who can help you, you won't be able to. If this little book helps even one family get there, I can die happy – there, that's my wish list!

I mentioned earlier that people fear they will not achieve what they want before they die. This is one of the things you can do in the ACP – you can make sure everyone knows what you/your child wants to achieve in the time you/they have left and it will lay the foundations for your family's memories after death. Nurse Becca told me that sometimes young people and families struggle to see what they have achieved. Her advice is to ask them to write or record, *in their own words and pictures*, their history – the important things that have happened in their lives. This can be significant or special events, social, health or educational. It's a way of recording and treasuring memories and then being able to celebrate them. This can then be shared, if they wish, with people important to them.

For young people, it is so important that their photos, videos and documents are saved across a number of devices and cloud-based platforms. Make sure you know which your child uses and that they have passed on passwords. The Digital Legacy Association, the professional body for digital assets and legacy in the UK, has great advice (and training for health professionals). There are death apps to help people curate their after life.[22] These apps allow people to give their family and loved ones unconditional control not only of their social media accounts after their death by digitally transmitting passwords, but also of online banking, shopping accounts and subscriptions. If you want your loved ones to have unconditional control of a social media account after your death, you will need to plan.

Some children and young people like to make an actual bucket list,[23] but that's a very personal choice. DD didn't but he did write out his own will (see below). (There's a social media

---

22   See, for example, www.safebeyond.com.
23   Leah's Bucket List online is a good example: www.shouldhavebeenamermaid.com/bucket-list.

will template available online.[24]) I think I feel a bucket list would have been too much pressure for us and we just wanted to take whatever each day offered. The wonderful thing is that there are lots of incredible organisations out there whose sole purpose is to fulfil wishes for very sick children and young people – I've put a short list in the Resources at the end of the book. Thank you to them all, as financially the burden of having a child this sick otherwise means that families would not be able to afford to fulfil them and make some incredible memories. Having those memories helps cope with the grief afterwards and could link to what you might want to do later as a legacy for your child.

Nothing is too small. Small is equally perfect. It could be a simple plaster cast of your baby's foot; parents have made joint plaster casts of their child's hand held within their own. You can have fingerprint jewellery made. The SiMBA charity has developed the most beautiful memory boxes which include imprint kits (see Other Useful Resources) and SANDS charity offers them free of charge to families and all healthcare professionals and providers (see Resources). Don't forget recordings – the sound of their voice is as unique as their picture or the smell of their clothes – as well as videos and photos.[25] I've even come across a gorgeous company in the UK – LoveKeepCreate – that makes cushions/teddies/blankets from their clothes as a keepsake (again, see Other Useful Resources). There are similar companies in the US.

A LIST OF WHO YOU WANT WITH YOU IN SUPPORT
Emotional and spiritual support

When it is clear that death is days away, who will you want with you? Which family members might want to say goodbye or stay and help?

---

24 See http://deadsocial.org.
25 See, for example, www.giftsofremembrance.co.uk.

Do you want any religious figures in support?

Make a list of important telephone numbers that family or health professionals can ring for you, including one for someone who can be with you very quickly if you suddenly need another pair of hands or you want younger children to be looked after.

You could also draw up a list of people you want family or a friend to contact after the death, so you don't have to do it. I found it invaluable having my sister as a 'briefing agent', who kept everyone up to date so we didn't have to repeat the same information over and over again.

Medical support

Draw up a list with your health professional of those you can call for different aspects of care, if you do not already have one. Nurse Becca Riley recommends drawing up a relationship circle so you can see who is important in your care.[26]

You should be provided with a number you can call 24/7 – especially important out of hours – for emergency medical advice and back-up. It's probably the health professional you're making this plan with, but there will be a rota so that if they're unavailable, someone always steps in. They will know who you are (crucial) and have a copy of your plan and can contact any member of your extensive medical team for advice on your behalf. They should also be able to deal with pharmacy issues for you or source equipment that might suddenly be required – for example, a commode (portable loo) or special mattress or oxygen.

In the US, hospice agencies can provide much of this equipment free and you can tailor services according to your need. They can provide a 24/7 number and RN to visit if you would prefer that to your oncologist/neurologist taking the call.

---

26   See Becca's toolkit (Appendix).

ORGAN/TISSUE DONATION AND BODY DONATION (INCLUDING BRAIN)[27]

Coming, as I do, from the brain tumour community, this is such an important section, but I know that there are also well over 600 neurodegenerative diseases of infancy stemming from structural abnormalities of the central nervous system (CNS). It is the rarity of many of these childhood conditions, many with no known cause, that makes research so vital in the search for answers and to develop desperately needed treatments and potential cures. DD's organs were not eligible to be given to save another child due to his metastasised cancer, so he could not have been a donor, and there are other medical conditions that mean you/your child's body cannot be accepted. I assume this was why I was not asked at our ACP meeting about donation. I'd really liked to have known about other types of donation for science and their different uses: anatomical research (medical students need to understand how anatomy works); research (to understand the mechanisms of disease and find cures); and education and training (for surgical techniques, for example).

I now understand that there is live tissue, often collected during surgery or by biopsy, but then there is also tissue collected after death, post-mortem. It is only in the last couple of years that samples of live tissue from children and young people's brain tumours have been systematically collected at diagnosis in the UK[28] to try to fill the huge gap in research for new treatments that will cause less harm and save more lives. However, not all children have surgery at the beginning; furthermore, when a brain cancer has metastasised – spread – it is then a *different cancer*. Even if tissue was collected from your child at the beginning, there is now a desperate need for live tissue from a biopsy that will show

---

27 There is separate registration in both the UK and US for organ/tissue donation for transplants as opposed to donating all or part (e.g. brain) of your/child's body to science. They are different things. I was not aware of this. All types require planning – conversations in advance – for the best chance of success.

28 The CCLG Tissue Bank systematically collects tissue from children and young people's brain tumours and sends them to a special tissue bank in the UK (www.cclg.org.uk/tissue-bank). This system does not yet exist in the US.

what happens to the brain when the cancer has spread, in order to develop new treatments. However, there is also the need for tissue collected after death. I have read such moving testimony from parents whose children have died from the untreatable, incurable DIPG brain tumours;[29] for them, donating their child's brain for research after their death represents their major hope and consoles them in their grief.

Knowing what I do now, this is probably what Toby and I would do if we had to make the decision today: organise to have DD's brain donated to science so that researchers could compare his tissue samples at diagnosis and then after death to understand how these horrific conditions progress. Months after he had died, once I realised how cross DD would have been, I contacted his doctors at Southampton Hospital to make sure that tumour samples from his original surgery had been sent to the tissue bank to be available for any research. They had, which was a huge relief. I also console myself with the fact we had organ donor registration forms and blood donation forms at his Celebration (see My Eulogy for DD) and lots of healthy people filled them in!

The practicalities of donation

- Whatever type of donation you are considering – for transplant and/or for science – it is important that you tell your medical team so they can help you organise it.

- For whole or partial body donation, including brain, making contact with medical colleges or brain banks before the death in order to talk through the practicalities of collecting and getting appropriate consents completed hugely increases the chances of success. You can also make sure you understand exactly what your/your child's tissue is being used for.

---

29 Diffuse intrinsic pontine gliomas (DIPG) are tumours found at the base of the brain. They are highly aggressive and median survival time is nine months from diagnosis.

In the UK, the Human Tissue Act of 2004 requires that written and witnessed consent is given prior to death if you wish to give part or the whole of your body to science. Consent for the donation of the brain of a child (who is anyone under the age of 18 for the purposes of the Human Tissue Act and under 16 in Scotland) can be given by the person themselves before they die, or if they have not made a decision before they died, a person with parental responsibility for them at the time of their death. The forms are on the website of the Human Tissue Authority (HTA).[30] The HTA licenses and inspects the organisations that collect/receive bodies for research to ensure that the network runs in an 'appropriate, respectful and well-managed way'.

- If you want to donate your/your child's brain, it is important that you make arrangements for the body to be retrieved. The ten brain banks currently operating in the UK all have different research remits and procedures for collection, but your team will easily be able to find out which would be suitable recipients for you/your child – Oxford's, for example, has a special interest in children and Brain UK accepts children's tissue post-mortem and has links to 90% of the NHS neuropathology centres (see 'Useful contacts' in the Resources). If you/your child is going to die at home/hospice, once the death has been certified the body will need to be transferred to a mortuary licensed by the HTA for the removal of the brain to take place;[31] the post-mortem needs to have been done within 24 hours of the death.

For the National Institutes of Health (NIH) NeuroBioBank process in the US, see link overleaf.

---

30 See www.hta.gov.uk. They also have FAQs and the list and contact details for all the medical colleges and the UK's tissue banks. In Scotland you need to check www.gov. scot/Topics/Health/Policy/BurialsCremation/BodyDonation.

31 All licensed mortuaries are listed on the HTA website: www.hta.gov.uk.

- After body or brain donation for science, medical colleges and brain banks usually cremate the body and hold a committal/memorial/thanksgiving service. You can request the body to be returned to you for private burial or cremation, although you would need to check if this is possible after whole-body donation. The NIH in the US make it clear in their FAQs that donation does not interfere with your funeral arrangements (again, see below).

- If your condition means you/your child are eligible to be an organ donor, be aware that this affects where you/your child can die – that is, your PoD choices. You have to be in hospital for the death in order to be prepared for and close to the operating theatres. Tissue – skin, bone, heart valves, eyes and tendons – can theoretically be donated after a home/hospice death in the UK, but there can be logistical issues in terms of making sure there is recent blood work to screen for infection, except in the case of eyes. You would therefore need to check with your team what is possible. The Organ Donor Register (ODR) is the best place to register wishes about donation: it allows people to record whether they wish to donate all, some or no organs and tissues after they have died.[32]

In the US, to be an organ donor, you can search online state by state for the organ donation registries which list the body donation programs and your medical team can contact an organ donor coordinator. They will usually review the situation and contact the family direct. You need to register separately if you wish to donate your child's brain or body to science. For brain donation, see https://neurobiobank.nih.gov. The Funeral Consumer's Alliance (FCA) also has useful information and links on its website (see 'Useful contacts' in the Resources).

---

32 See also HTA's Code F: Donation of solid organs and tissue for transplantation; www.organdonation.nhs.uk has information and FAQs.

LAYING OUT AND FUNERAL ARRANGEMENTS AND THE WILL

Given our emotional state after our child has died, if you haven't thought about it – and we hadn't – you will not know what choices are open to you and are more likely to just go along with whatever your health professional happens to know rather than what's available. This may or may not be what you or your child would actually want. Unfortunately, health professionals supporting us in hospital or at home at present are not always aware of your legal rights as a parent with regard to all the choices available. This effectively means that many parents, like my husband and me, were misinformed. I can't imagine this would ever be deliberate; it certainly wasn't in our case – simply lack of knowledge. Just one example I heard recently was of a family being told by nurses in hospital that their child *had* to be embalmed – this is totally untrue.

Having spoken to the mortuary service at Southampton General Hospital, the inescapable conclusion I came to is that if you have thought about plans for after the death and included them in your ACP and your medical team is aware, it makes everything easier to deliver smoothly, especially if you're planning a DIY funeral without a funeral director (see Chapter 5). Reading any kind of written material just after your child has just died is virtually impossible. So this is my plea to you – don't skip this section!

In the US, some states – namely, Alabama, Connecticut, Illinois, Indiana, Louisiana, Michigan, Nebraska, New Jersey and New York – have restrictions on your ability to care for your dead yourself, so if you live in one of these states, you will need to contact them for laws and regulations governing the practice of mortuary science.[33] The time between last breath and final resting is referred to as funeral care, so home funeral care is the family doing this at home rather than professionals at a funeral director's.

---

33 *Final Rights: Reclaiming the American Way of Death* by Joshua Slocum and Lisa Carlson (Upper Access, 2011) gives a state-by-state overview.

Laying out a body (see Chapter 5) refers to preparing a body for the funeral – washing and dressing the body – and the emotional and religious/spiritual rites associated with this. Here are some questions to consider.

Whom do you want handling their body and transferring them?

- The undertaker at a funeral director's. You can choose a funeral director and contact them in advance. Do ring more than one – there are small family-run businesses or large corporates. Ask for cost estimates and remember you don't have to accept all the options presented.[34]

- Yourself/family/religious figures. There is no law to say a family cannot transport their child themselves and there is no legal requirement to use a funeral director. This is also the case in most states in the US (see note above about restrictions).

- Or a mixture. Some funeral directors are very flexible about this (see Chapter 5).

Where do you want your child's body to be before the funeral/celebration?

Best practice is to aim to transfer a child from their PoD within four to six hours of death, but there is actually no legal obligation in the UK. The choices are:

- at the funeral director's

- in a hospice cool room, if one is available locally

- at home

---

34 www.funeralzone.co.uk/NHS has a 'compare funeral directors' section and is a free online resource. The US Funeral Consumer's Alliance (FCA) is their equivalent (see Resources).

- in a hospital mortuary.

If the PoD is a hospital, staff will try to give you as much privacy and time as possible to be with your child after death, but we cannot ignore the underlying pressure for beds in our busy NHS or in the US. If there's a big queue of children needing to be admitted, clearly you will not get much time. This is not the case in the UK with stillbirth or neonatal death; there are facilities for both parents to stay as long as you need unless you wish to go straight home or to a hospice cool room with your baby.

The mortuary at the hospital is a transition point for your child rather than anywhere they stay for any length of time, unless you decide otherwise; they just need to be admitted, as you would in any ward, and then released, provided death certification has happened and you have something suitable for the body to be transported in safely in the car if you're not using a funeral director (see Chapter 5). This does not have to take long if staff know your plans in advance. In practical terms, you can only avoid the mortuary totally with a baby in a Moses basket as they can be carried straight from the ward to the car. (A mosquito net is suggested for privacy for the baby's body, if you wish.[35]) For children and young people, you would need to get a stretcher out to the car park, and transferring your child's body through a busy hospital and into a public car park is not recommended when you can park right by the door of the mortuary and have some privacy.

If your hospital's mortuary has the facilities to help you lay out your child (Southampton's does, for example), you could arrange to have your child stay there and then go direct to the funeral. Just ask to see if it's possible.

If the PoD is a hospice, it's simpler. They have special temperature control for the room where a child dies, which means the body can stay there until the funeral if you wish, or you could ask for the body to go home until the funeral (see

---

35 *Collaborative guidance for staff to support families who wish to take their baby home after death,* NHS Scotland and Children's Hospice Association Scotland (CHAS).

below). You can go back home and make arrangements with the rest of your family and community and come back to the hospice whenever you want if you suddenly need to see your child during this time – even at 2am! Or you can stay with them at the hospice with the rest of the family if you wish.

If the PoD is home, you can do what you want! If you decide you want your child to stay at home until the funeral rather than going to the hospice or funeral director, due to inevitable changes in their body after death (*please* read the section 'Changes to the body' in Chapter 5), you will need a portable cooling unit (see Chapter 5). Some hospices have these to lend out to families for this purpose.

Funeral[36]

We normally think of a funeral as an event or ceremony honouring the person who has died, together with a cremation or burial. The main thing is to realise that you don't have to do them *together*. You can have a burial or cremation and not have an accompanying ceremony. The ceremony can be held at a later date or not at all if that is what you wish. There are no laws governing funerals; there is only a legal duty to dispose of the body in the UK, either by burial or cremation.

I recently listened to the most fantastic interview of a young woman, in her mid-20s, whose brain tumour had returned yet again, and this time it was going to kill her. She robustly made it clear that she didn't want anyone to assume what she would like at her funeral. She wanted to have it all discussed and written down, so that she could be sure her wishes were going to be respected and she was clearly enjoying doing so.

I know it is totally agonising for us, the parents, but the evidence from young people online and off is very clear: they often want and need to be able to discuss it. Be aware that older children and young people are worried about upsetting us

---

36 There are loads of creative ideas online and off. See, for example, www.goodfuneralguide.co.uk.

parents, so may not be able to bring it up with you directly and may instead ask their medical team or someone at the hospice they trust, to ask you (see Julia's story below). There is lots of evidence online for young people using their digital skills to honour and remember someone who has died; this could be really helpful if you have an older child who is going to die and who can create this with their friends and siblings. If you search under 'memorial websites' or 'virtual memorials', you can find websites where you can create your own page and fill it with videos, pictures, virtual candles, a guest book and tributes. Some are free. For those of us less adept at navigating social media sites, there are now organisations that can help curate online legacy after death.[37]

Note on funeral costs

They are frankly horrendous, particularly if your family has been struggling for years with complex palliative needs for your child or extended cancer treatment, as we did. Costs change, so I didn't think it helpful to put them down. As a general rule, the simpler the funeral, the more you do yourself, the less expensive. I have included details in 'Useful contacts' in the Resources about organisations in the UK that can help with costs. In the UK, many funeral directors do offer their basic services free of charge if the child has died under the age of 16. This usually means the costs of organising the funeral and coffin, but does not include the cars, flowers and extra services. There are campaigns underway in the UK for child funeral costs to be free and for bereavement leave for parents – support them!

In the US, there are very strong non-profit organisations advising the public on their legal rights and how to get the most cost-effective service, which started after the Great Depression. Access the Funeral Consumer's Alliance (FCA) website to find

---

37 For example, www.thedigitalbeyond.com is a digital death and afterlife online services list.

your local group (see Resources). Hospitals often have funds to help families; your social worker should be able to help you access these.

HOW IT WORKED FOR US AND OTHERS

Our ACP meeting was held, at our request, at home in the week following DD's incurable diagnosis. It took over an hour and it was only me, the paediatric palliative specialist nurse from Southampton General Hospital (our key worker or go-to professional) and a lot of cups of tea. I can't remember why Toby wasn't there, whether he was at work or with all the children. DD didn't want to know about the medication details – he understood the outline – and I didn't want him to have to hear what I was worried about in case that worried him! Also, his dementia meant his short-term memory was already eroding. I wish I had a video of myself in order to be able to show you proof of my relief afterwards. I felt kilos lighter as the weight of most of my fear and worry lifted. Knowing what I do now, I also wish I had been put in touch with Together for Short Lives so I could have identified what services were available to us locally.

My main fears were (1) pain, (2) seizures and (3) that someone would cart him off to hospital, but then there's the lesser but still important fear that you somehow won't be there when your child actually dies.

- To deal with pain, the nurse arrived with a shedload of medication, in various different forms: pills that can be swallowed and then injectable forms in case they can't swallow or if DD was vomiting. (We had major form with the last symptom; DD's doctor is on record saying he was the sickiest brain tumour patient they had ever had, but it was got under control completely with medication.) She explained any of the unfamiliar ones, double-checked I knew always to keep to his regular schedule for pain relief but to give more *in advance* if I thought some activity was likely to increase his pain. I could always ring for detailed advice from the pain team at the hospital if I was worried.

- Another shed-load of medication was for seizures, again in different forms. (The kitchen shelf was a pharmacist's stockroom.) I was freaked out by the form of the syringe for the main medication. So, to reassure me, she got one out of its packet and showed me how it worked. If he had a seizure, I was to give him one dose and then five minutes later, if it hadn't worked, I was to give him another. If that didn't work, I was to call an ambulance.

- This neatly led to my terror of him being taken by the ambulance to hospital, against his and our wishes. Astonished, she replied: 'Oh that's easy, we just sign one of these forms and I flag up this telephone number on the local 999 system. Then they know that they're only coming here to stabilise him and support you until further help arrives – they can put in an intravenous line for pain or seizures if necessary.'

She filled out a load of paperwork and then remarked, 'It's so much easier to make a plan when you know what the family wants!'

I didn't actually manage to mention my fear of DD dying without Toby and me being with him, but I think that's because I knew there was nothing anyone could do about it. We were back to hoping we got lucky (bearing in mind our gorgeous child seemed to have had an astonishing run of appalling luck).

The last bit of the meeting was our nurse being sure I knew whom to call and when. I was instructed to call her every Friday morning, first thing, to say how DD was doing. She would then go straight to the multi-disciplinary team (MDT) meeting afterwards to update all DD's doctors. If I had any questions, she would ask and then get straight back to me when action had been decided. DD took great pleasure the first time in instructing me what to tell her to tell the team: 'He's not dead yet!'

My sister was very important in terms of linking us to all our friends and community, and so she was instrumental in ensuring DD's wishes were fulfilled. Since very early on, she had a list of emails and would send out fairly regular updates, so everyone knew what was happening, they could check with her if they were unsure, and as a result there was no misinformation. (People asked at the beginning if they could tell their children the truth if they wanted to know. We said, yes, if they've asked and need to know, tell them.) She's also a genius at organisation, so I would delegate anything requiring this to her. Talking on the phone about such distressing news is utterly exhausting and I learned quickly I could not afford to waste energy doing this. I also had to learn to ask for help with *everything* and that, far from me being thought a failure, people loved being told what they could do! So once everyone knew DD had little time left, a flood of emails flowed offering help and suggesting other wonderful things to do.

If you're reading this in order to support a family, my top tip would be ask a direct question to which a yes/no answer is all that's required but leaving them an opt-out so that they don't feel obliged – for example, 'Would you like a lasagne dropped round tonight or is your fridge jammed already?'

DD's plans included: a summer party in the garden with all his mates; flying hawks; tending his bees regularly; going to the school prom (the Rays of Sunshine charity paid for him to be picked up with his friends in a huge limousine); and eating delicious food all the time. I was always being given 'constructive criticism' for how the meal could be improved the next time, which drove me mad. Holly was certainly not going to let her brother waste any opportunity for fun. He tried to go up for a rest one afternoon, after a fantastic lunch out with lots of close friends, but she refused to let him and pestered him to come and play with her outside.

Holly: Come on, DD, pleease, don't be so boring!

DD: No. I must go up; I've got to have my rest.

Holly: But you can rest when you're dead.

DD [pauses mid-stairs and looks down at his little sister]: Oh, all right then. Let's go!

He came down and they went outside to play on the lawn, leaving me open-mouthed with horror. Of course, she was right, and DD and I knew it.

This reminds me how very many times I found myself ashamed at my lack of courage compared with DD; just who was the grown-up? It was so embarrassing. DD drew up his own will one afternoon and Holly wandered into his room and asked what he was doing. He told her and asked if there was anything of his she wanted, so she started pointing at various things in his room. That DD would write a will hadn't occurred to me; I had no idea it was going on until Holly came bouncing into the kitchen and announced gleefully she was getting all his jellybeans. It certainly meant no sibling arguments after he had died, as it was all written down. I think his funeral/celebration plans would have been next, but his dementia took over. He hadn't mentioned anything to Holly, but Rufus has just told me that the only thing he said was that he didn't want it to be 'f**cking boring'! (Apologies – unlike his mother, DD rarely swore.)

Michelle and Keir

Michelle summarises that Keir's plan on paper was ostensibly just 'what to do if he has a sudden collapse' – an emergency. It did not cover all the areas that I have outlined. Here she describes this in more detail:

The advance care plan for children (as it is today) was still in its infancy when Keir was diagnosed. Dan, our community paediatrician and voice of reason,[38] came to our house carrying this document called a Personal Resuscitation Plan which he said we could discuss either at that time or it could wait until

---

38 See 'Parallel planning' in Chapter 1.

we felt more able. Though thinking about it, how do you ever feel 'more able' to discuss what you want to happen when your child dies? The thought is quite rightly, so alien, to most people. At first, Keir's plan was for full resuscitation – at any cost. The reason for this is that even though we had been given the cold hard facts about his condition – he *will* deteriorate, he *will* die – we still didn't fully believe it. He'll be the one to defy all the odds and survive this terrible disease.

Michelle explained to me that by becoming an expert in everything to do with Keir's care – including becoming a 'demon chest physio' – he only ever needed to be hospitalised four times. We both believe that *less hospital = more life*! Then in August 2012, the second time, admitted for poor oxygen saturation, everything started to go wrong after he was finally given IV antibiotics:

> The consultant on duty asked me what I wanted to do if he didn't start to respond. I went into full-on panic mode. I rang Martin (who was at work) and told him that he needed to get to the hospital as the doctors wanted to talk to us in the dreaded 'quiet room'. When he arrived, we spoke to the doctors. Despite previously wanting everything done, including ventilation, we arrived at the conclusion that this wouldn't be right for him. (Much to Erin's complete incredulity. In her 15-year-old mind, why would we not do everything we could to keep our child alive? When it finally happened, she not only understood but was part of the decision-making process.) We would only be doing it for ourselves. We agreed to non-invasive treatment via CPAP (continuous positive airway pressure) which can only be described as akin to sticking your head out of a fast-moving car in a Force 10 gale. Not pleasant. And so began the longest weeks of our lives up to that point.
>
> Long story short, he made it through and we had another wonderful, precious 18 months with him. We had already made lots of memories with him throughout his illness. We started to photograph and video more and more. We had completed the

obligatory trip to Disneyland, though our subsequent holidays to the South West (usually Cornwall or Dorset) were the ones that meant the most. We laughed lots and we worried lots, but the memories we made continue to be vital to our ongoing struggle with grief. Keir continued to go to school throughout his illness, though the frequency of his school week was adjusted as he grew more tired. He *loved* music so many of our memories revolve around making music. He had friends who visited him. He spent a lot of time with my dad reading, laughing and doing crafts. He was happy.

Julia and Kimberley[39]

Kimberley had asked a carer at her hospice to let her mum know she wanted to talk about her funeral with her. Julia admits: 'One of the hardest things I ever had to do was to talk to her about her funeral'. Kimberley had written down her wishes in a letter she wanted Julia to read but:

> I kept saying 'in a minute', as I really didn't want to read it. Eventually, I knew I had to because it was what she wanted, and if she was brave enough to write this letter and discuss it then I had to be big enough to face it too... [Also] we didn't want to regret that we had got it wrong by missing something vital out. Planning gives you time to get it right...

Here Julia describes finally making herself go through the letter of wishes Kimberley had written with her:

> Kimbers was adamant about what she wanted; and what she didn't. Her wishes were really detailed: not having her hair in a toggle, no slides; how she wanted the coffin inside and out; the horse and carriage; everyone wearing pink, even the boys; who was to carry the coffin; that her brothers sing 'Dream a Little Dream'; she wanted Black Eye Peas music but we could pick

---

39 *Lives Worth Living: Fifteen Stories of Exceptional Children Whose Short Lives Left a Lasting Legacy*, pp.88–96.

the rest; strawberries and bubbly to be served after the service. She wanted to leave Teddy for us to look after… We cried when we read her requests, but once we had finished I said we were going to put it in a box and lock it away. I also told her that if she wanted to add anything to it or talk about it again, she just had to say.

Theresa and Asher

Theresa did not have a formal ACP drawn up in the form we have them in the UK, but she says that 'our wishes were clearly documented in his medical charts and his doctors wrote orders to ensure they were followed'.

> After 2011, when Asher had decided not to have the operation and was discharged, he continued to spend weeks in hospital. Each time we had the conversation and set a DNR – and we had it many times when Asher was admitted and discharged in the two years before his death – the 'menu items' we chose became less and less aggressive and included fewer interventions. Sometimes the admissions were severe with intubation and medically induced coma, other times he just needed a bit of antibiotics and respiratory support. In those cases, we would change the DNR to more aggressive interventions because he didn't 'seem so sick'. It's a horrendous roller-coaster ride that I would never wish on any parent.

Decisions now were always guided by looking at his life from a 'do for, not to' perspective.

She describes how they lived those years:

> That's not a typo – I mean it: We *lived*. More beach time, horseback riding, roller coasters, it was *awesome*!

Then Theresa explains how the 'tune-ups' in PICU became ever more frequent and lasted longer:

It was so hard on him. Asher was known for his smile and laugh (and curly brown hair). His nickname was the Ambassador of Happiness! I distinctly remember the moment we all began to come to terms that he really was dying (although I'm not sure we ever actually said the 'D' word out loud). He was in the PICU for one of his more 'aggressive tune-ups' and had been intubated. Prior to this admission, if he was intubated, he would pop back rather quickly. I even have pictures of him laughing and smiling *while he had a tube down his throat!* This time was markedly different. He came off the ventilator and his demeanour was just pure exhaustion. His eyes were so sad. No smiling. No laughing. One of his doctors immediately noticed this. 'He doesn't look like Asher. He looks so tired.' That's when we knew. Intubation was not doing something *for* Asher any more; instead, intubation was doing something *to* him. After January 2013, he was never intubated again.

Alison and Ryan

When I asked Alison whether they had good parallel planning and advance care planning for Ryan, I was staggered at the level of support she received, particularly from their hospice. Great care was taken to ensure that detailed plans were kept updated for his end-of-life care and support, and counselling was given to the family by the hospice team *at every stage.* The GP would visit them weekly at home and their consultant would be available via telephone to liaise with the hospice staff if needed. It was a roller-coaster with peaks and then near-death troughs, as with many of these complex conditions, but in the event Ryan lived nearly three times longer than they were first told to expect.

Not only were the plans in place for Ryan's end-of-life care before death, but Alison and her husband were given the support necessary for them to be able to plan in advance for after Ryan's death, for his funeral arrangements, which I so wish I had been able to do. So twelve months *before* Ryan finally died, Alison met their funeral director: 'It was horrendous, it was so hard, as you'd expect. I felt horrible; was I speeding up his death?' But then the help and information that the funeral director supplied were instrumental in making her aware of the choices available to the family in order for her to make the right decisions for them. As Alison says, 'It enabled us to make decisions whilst our minds were not in a complete grieving state.' So having initially planned to have a home death, Alison changed her mind and decided that going to the hospice to be with the team they all knew so well was best for them as they would be able to provide support for her husband and little Rhys. She worried that there might be a break in pain relief for Ryan out in the community, but, just as important, she didn't want community banging on the door or to have to answer the phone; she didn't want the family to be disturbed, so they could focus on their last special time with Ryan. She summarises: 'Knowing that these decisions were done, we were able to concentrate on things that were important to us.'

Jane and Callum

I asked Jane when parallel planning for Callum's end-of-life care was first introduced and she told me that it was never formally introduced. The hospice where they received respite care over the years did ask her, many years before Callum died, to 'think about the process and what I might want from it'. She did revisit this annually. It was called the 'spirituality tour', which sounds encouraging, but then Jane went on to say:

> There's a lot of work to be done in producing a sensitive yet practical ACP that can be accessed and understood by everyone. It is too easy for HCPs to forget that families often don't understand what is written and…communicating in medicalese adds unnecessary stress.

So Jane says she had an ACP, which was one 'in my own thoughts', addressing the emotional and practical issues, and one more medical one. It is these plans she credits with 'helping me to provide the passing for Callum that he deserved'. She also achieved the most brilliant day with him indoor sky-diving and skiing, and recorded him on a precious video. Jane hadn't realised this was even possible for a severely disabled child in a wheelchair until, dropping off his older brother Connor at one of these activity centres one day, she just happened to ask. Callum wasn't able to speak but expressed his feelings by laughing all the way home in the car!

Chapter 3

THE LAST TWO WEEKS (ROUGHLY)

WHAT'S CHANGED?

Parents recognise when a stable phase comes to an end. If you have been caring for your child for a long time, you have learned to identify even very subtle variation in patterns of symptoms and behaviour which you report to your medical team. Essentially, everything starts to ramp up: symptoms, decisions, medication, health and social care professionals' input and tiredness/exhaustion. You know it's coming, whether you have acknowledged it or not. If you haven't, your body feels it. Unpredictability and therefore reduced expectations rule: it's very much living day by day. However, I still consider this phase *living*; DD was not yet dying – he was very, very ill.

ANTICIPATORY GRIEF

You start to grieve the instant you are told that your child has a life-shortening or incurable condition. The word 'grief' comes from the Old French *grever*, which literally means to burden, afflict, oppress, and that in turn comes from the Latin word *gravare* – to make heavy. What made my chest feel as heavy as lead was the knowledge that time with DD was now very short and we would never get it back. I wrestled with how on earth I was supposed to enjoy DD's party when I knew it was his last, *ever*. No more birthdays, no graduation, no wedding, no christenings. In the last fortnight, it felt like a series of lasts

– the last walk outside, the last time he spoke, the last time he managed to get upstairs. *Agony* is the only word I can find for the level of pain.

I wish someone had told me that this is 'normal' and is called anticipatory grief, because I started to think either I was mad or pathetic that I couldn't keep a grip, or both. Whatever it was, I knew I needed to keep my head under control, as I was determined not to ruin the little time left and then have spoiled future memories. I needed to shut down my imagination like Sir Ranulph (Chapter 1) and not allow the thought: this is his *last* anything. I had to get very fierce with my head. What I'm talking about is living totally in the present.

That was easy to type but *so hard to do*.

My next admission is probably the ugliest and worst. I got to the point where seeing him physically and mentally disintegrate became so unbearable that I thought: 'Why can't he just die now, right this minute? I can't stand it one more second.' Then I felt sick with guilt. Did I want his suffering to cease for him or for me? The honest answer is for the both of us. I couldn't bear the idea of him leaving and not seeing/hearing/smelling him anymore, but I equally couldn't stand seeing him suffer. *Excruciating* is the word and the emotion is wrecking and exhausting. This leads neatly to the next heading.

COPING[1] AND RESPITE

It's cruel that at the very time when you need to be good at taking decisions, you are almost certainly exhausted and super-stressed. It gets to the point where you are too tired even to see what should be done – something I hope friends or health professionals are looking out for, so they can step in. This is where having made all the major decisions at the advance care

---

1   For HCPs interested in how parents cope, this article may be of interest: Darlington, A.E., Korones, D.N. and Norton, S.A. (2017) 'Parental coping in the context of having a child who is facing death: A theoretical framework.' *Palliative and Supportive Care* *13*:1–10.

plan meeting (see Chapter 2) really pays off. You will also be at a distinct advantage if you already have a relationship with a hospice because giving the family breaks – respite – is built into everything they do. It's even more important at the end of life because it is so hard. When I say breaks, it can just be going out for a walk, alone, with your dog for half an hour and someone sitting with your child and their siblings. The mental pain of going through this leads to physical pain and everyone has a breaking point. *Anything* that relieves the relentless pressure on you, even for a few minutes, is gold dust.

Please don't think you should have to be present with your child 24 hours a day, seven days a week. I did think that at the beginning, I thought that's what a mother's supposed to do with a very sick child. It took about six months before I realised that it wasn't just impractical, but it was actually dangerous for DD and Holly and Rufus! I became so tired that my decision making was impaired and then I made a mistake with DD's medication. Panicked calls to the hospital followed. I could also easily have crashed the car with all three children in it. I realised that to be a good carer and nurse I needed to look after myself, and that was not easy to do because essentially I didn't care about myself. You cannot do this on your own, nor should you. I had that experience to guide me at DD's end of life, which boiled down to ensuring that our family life continued as normally as possible. If the sick child becomes The Priority, then the siblings suffer and their behaviour deteriorates and family life suffers and then the sick child suffers more. The same applies to the parents' relationship. It's not just about the sick child. Hospices understand this very well and therefore look after the whole family.

Over the five years, I learned the hard way to pace myself. First warning sign was a rising pressure in my chest and an overwhelming sense that things were going to get away from me. Some people feel it more in their stomachs. This was the time for me not to talk too much, pare everything back to total essentials, make sure I was going to sleep (i.e. take my prescribed sleeping pills) and *tell* someone. I found a hot water bottle against the heart was good, or really fierce bear hugs, or the breathing exercise in the box below. If I'd not paid attention or ignored the signs, the red alert sign was a panic attack – there's your body's natural fuse box popping a switch or two or three, and you need to make sure the main breaker switch doesn't go. Symptoms included clammy, cold sweat all over, nausea, shallow breathing, faintness, pain and weakness in an arm. It's extremely unpleasant and the first time I actually thought I *was* having a heart attack until I figured I'd be dead already!

I love the fact that the word 'cope' comes from the ancient Greek *kolaphos*, meaning a blow with the fist; in Old French, we then find *colp*, meaning a blow, with a corresponding verb *colper*, which leads to our Middle English sense of to meet in battle or come to blows. I wish I had looked this up before, because it makes so much sense: the body blows of grief. It's the fight part of fight or flight. I could have just smacked everyone when they asked me how I was coping – childish, I know, but how satisfying! Until I had no friends left and then I really wouldn't have coped!

BREATHING EXERCISE

Put one hand at the level of your abdomen and imagine that the air that is going to fill your lungs is coming in from there, not in your mouth. (This is to help visualise our breath low down instead of high up in our shoulders, which shouldn't move.) As you breathe, you're going to move your other hand up to indicate the air filling up your lungs from the bottom and then reverse this when you breathe out. Try to visualise the air filling your lung-tank and expelling it, like a bellows. I found the hardest bit controlling the intake – it needs to be s-l-o-w; stress would make my body seize the air instead of draw it in gradually.

Ready:

- Purse your lips as if you have a straw or, better still, get one.

- You're going to breathe in slowly over a count of four, moving your hand up.

- Hold your breath for a count of four (relax!).

- Then breathe out over a count of four, moving your hand back down.

- Do this three times and then try to breathe in over a count of five, then six and so on.

This should have got your body off red alert.

SAYING GOODBYE

This is an interesting section for me as I know we all think this is what we're supposed to do. But are we? You see people in movies coming to say goodbye to someone who is dying, I've read about it and people came to try to say goodbye to my father in the last few weeks of his life. I say *try* because he was so cross that nobody dared! I'm assuming any psychologist reading this section is going to have a field day…

Saying goodbye – it always makes me think about the beautiful Cole Porter song 'Ev'ry Time We Say Goodbye, I Die a Little'. He wrote it in 1944 and I think of all those lovers saying goodbye during the War and not knowing if they would ever see each other again. 'Goodbye' in a society more religious than now would still have carried the imprint of its 16th-century meaning of God-be-with-you to keep their beloved safe. Maybe that's the difference: hope? There was a chance in the War that the lovers would be reunited, whereas with my child it was hopeless to say it unless I happened to be religious and believed in meeting in the afterlife. I do not have that luxury of belief. I do know, however, that my child did not want his parents to be hopeless and unable to live after he was gone because he said so: 'You and Dad will be okay? Won't you?' Therefore, I did not say goodbye, which means in my own warped logic that I cannot 'die a little' because he didn't want me to! I know it would not have helped me. I'll admit to denial, a horse refusing at a vast fence – I did not want DD to leave, ever, and therefore instinctively those words were never going to issue out of my maternal mouth because I refused to take my leave of him. And to me he still is with me. For me, saying 'I love you' was right; saying 'goodbye' was not. However, it is totally personal and there are no rules, as I keep saying!

I was totally taken aback when a mother rang before DD's party to ask if her son was expected to say goodbye to him. Her son was understandably apprehensive about what was expected of him at this 'party' for a dying friend. I hesitated, feeling very uncomfortable about making this decision, whilst understanding perfectly why this mother had rung. I ended up saying something along the lines of: 'I think DD would think that saying goodbye was weird, but if it feels right and your son finds himself saying it, then so be it.' To my knowledge, no one did because everyone was partying – it was not an ending! They may have said it as a figure of speech as they left, as you do, but not in a deliberate, this-is-the-last-time-I'm-going-to-see-you-ever sort of way. I don't honestly think at that point his friends believed it.

I understand that saying goodbye gives 'closure' – but to whom? To the dying child or young person who seems to be so much better than adults at living in the present? Is it more for the grown-ups and those left behind? Should I have explained to DD before his dementia really took hold that people needed to take their leave of him? I don't know and it's definitely too late now! As parents, Toby and I had the 'closure' that comes when someone is diagnosed with an aggressive illness that, despite everyone's best efforts, cannot be stopped. When I hear of parents fighting for 'closure' after the death of their child, usually when they don't know what actually happened, I feel so intensely for them because I understand how important it is in the struggle to understand what has happened to a piece of your own soul.

DD certainly never felt the need to say goodbye, but I realise his dementia does complicate that. However, his fascination with the Buddhist idea that you never leave but are recycled makes me think he would grin and say that goodbye is irrelevant. But that's just him, us. You must do what you need to do, when you need to. I think there's going and seeing someone knowing it's for the last time and then actually saying goodbye.

SYMPTOMS' CONTROL

Given there are roughly 390 different life-shortening conditions in children and young people and I'm not a health professional, I'm going to hand you over to professional advice in the form of CCLG's leaflet on the subject.[2] Warning: it is a long list of very unpleasant symptoms and your child is highly unlikely to have many of them, which means that it's probably less distressing to ask your medical team what you should expect at this point and how to manage it. They will know; it is something medical professionals are good at and comfortable discussing. Ours certainly were and DD's medical situation was very complex.

HOW IT WORKED FOR US AND OTHERS

DD's last fortnight was marked by acceleration in the medication needed to control his sickness and nausea and pain. Doses were larger and more frequent; I was on the phone to our nurse at the hospital for advice a lot, but it worked. On top of that, he started to have seizures. These were not the violent ones I was expecting and therefore the first time I didn't realise what was happening. I found out later they are called absence seizures because the

2   'Managing Symptoms at Home.' Can be downloaded at www.cclg.org.uk/publications/ search/managing/Managing-symptoms-at-home/PALLCARE.

patient is awake but doesn't appear to be able to hear and doesn't respond when you talk to them. DD's first one must have lasted for about ten minutes (which felt like hours) with him sitting utterly silent, just staring. I sat with him, to keep him safe, and decided to talk to him normally in case he could hear me. I had no idea if he would ever come back to me. So you can imagine my shock when after ten minutes he suddenly looked at me and said, 'What's for tea, Mum?' I'm not sure who needed medication more at that point! My GP called these 'events' and I would always ring and tell the team when he had one. We were lucky, though, when I consider the children I knew from hospital who were having dozens of seizures a day with severe epilepsy – DD only had a handful over this fortnight.

His short-term memory had almost completely gone by this point and his long-term was eroding fast. This meant that he still remembered he had cancer (he'd had it quarter of his life by this point) but had forgotten he was going to die, except that he knew something really important had happened. The result? He kept asking on a six-minute loop if he was having more cancer treatment. I would reply, 'No', and then he'd look really startled and say, 'Am I going to die?' He did this for a good week. I got so desperate that I contemplated lying and saying, no, he wasn't dying – at my sister's suggestion – but I was too scared that at some level that would deeply confuse him because he had processed it at the time, and if I suddenly changed the narrative now, he might get distressed. It was too risky. He kept asking Rufus what his GCSE exam choices were. Holly was the only one who escaped the *Groundhog Day* questions and, as usual, took sisterly advantage. Sitting on our bed all watching a movie one evening, DD comes out of the shower room dripping wet, wrapped in a towel, and then says moments later, 'Have I had a shower?' Quick as a flash, Holly says, 'No'.

We were now housebound as DD didn't know what was going on and had forgotten who a lot of people were, but crucially his body seemed to know where it was and seemed to be on its own happy autopilot. For example, his body knew exactly how many steps from his bedroom to the bathroom and so on. Therefore, going elsewhere would have confused and then distressed him. This is why decamping to a hospice would have been inappropriate for him but hospice homecare would have been perfect.

Anyone who is familiar with dementia in a loved one knows that it is very uneven; the disintegration does not happen on an even, downward trajectory – it seems to fluctuate up and down on its downward slide. Just when you think that an entire section of their knowledge has vanished into the ether, they suddenly say something so profound, so wise, that it is shattering and amazing and inspiring. A girlfriend reminded me the other day, tearing up, that DD had suddenly grasped the arm of her daughter, a close friend of his, when they were out walking in that last fortnight and said, 'You know you're amazing, don't you?' Fifteen-year-old girls don't tend to think that and she's never forgotten it.

But I'm not going to pretend it wasn't the hardest thing I've ever had to bear. I can't unlearn the day we were cooking together side by side (cooking was perfect as I could keep showing him what he was supposed to be doing and the tasks are simple and sensory: shelling peas, cutting fresh mint, crushing garlic) and he suddenly looked at me, smiling, and said, 'You look very like my mum'. My sense of humour always rescues me in my darkest hour and I found myself grinning back and saying, 'Yes, I certainly do. She's marvellous!' Two minutes later he was back, but I knew it was only a question of time. I found a Tweet sent at that time (I was trying to raise awareness of the HeadSmart campaign and the plight of children in the UK with late-diagnosed brain tumours):

[7 August] DD's Nimble Neurology: mix of film, bk, thought, dream, curriculum, feeling all coming out unedited. Hell of a mental ride.

We needed new equipment. Locals rallied when I posted that DD was wandering at night – he'd forget if it was day or night and that he'd gone to bed – and Toby and I were terrified he would fall down the stairs. So someone pitched up with a child stairgate. By this time Toby had told me I was too tired to cope at night, so our team contacted the Marie Curie charity for night nursing. This meant I could take half a lorazepam and sleep, leaving me with enough strength in the day. Friends came and stayed, bringing their own bed linen, to help cook, clean, garden, take Rufus and Holly to friends for trips or stay with DD, so I could go on a bike ride. However distressed and stressed, I always felt better after that half-hour exercise. Alongside massage and a half-hour afternoon nap, I found it was the best 'medication' for coping.

In general, when I look back and consider how ill DD was, it is amazing that most of the medical help we needed at this time was advice, which could be given on the phone. Our district nurse came and introduced herself on her way home with her gorgeous little boy in tow; our GP popped in after work a couple of times after DD had a seizure, as he lived very locally; and the Marie Curie nurse (we had two) came around nine o'clock at night, most nights. Other nights were covered by my aunt, who also lived locally. I know how lucky we were to have this community support.

However, I'd be lying if I didn't say it did feel at the time we were *only just* on top of it. Toby and I started talking about getting more day help, as DD could not be left for a nanosecond because of his wandering and lack of balance from his spinal tumours and neurological issues, and we still needed to try to give Holly and Rufus a summer holiday. This would have been where hospice care at home would have been perfect if we had been signposted to it. It was the speed of acceleration in his decline that was hard to manage; hardly had I got his medication right and it would need to be changed and upped again following yet another detailed phone conversation with our team at the hospital, and I would have to draw up yet another drugs schedule to be sure we kept on top of everything.

Michelle and Keir

I knew that this time it was different. I had noticed that Keir had recently started to look uncomfortable in his chair which was a bespoke seat moulded just for him. He had always looked so comfortable and we worked really hard with the OT, physio and Baldy Simon (the super-ace wheelchair engineer) to make sure he had the best and most supportive seating. In my opinion, this is something that should never be neglected as it kept our boy well for much longer than expected. (By the way, Baldy Simon knew we called him Baldy Simon. I don't think he minded as when I said it at our regular wheelchair clinic appointments, Keir would howl with laughter and, after all, he was the customer and the customer is always right!) But his demeanour had changed; he looked uncomfortable and tired and now his heart was being a right royal pain in the arse. We had started to say goodbye at that June appointment in 2005, but now it was staring us right in the face.

The final acute episode came just before Christmas 2013 and Keir was gearing up for his (what came to be expected) pre-Christmas chest infection. He had his flu jab every year and was always perfectly fine after it – in fact, the GP used to come out to the car park to administer it so that we didn't have to get him out of the car in the cold. My GPs are wonderful! Anyway, Keir liked to keep us on our toes: will he be in hospital for Christmas or will he be well enough to be discharged just prior? It was an unpleasant game we had become accustomed to.

This time was different, though. After our first scare in August 2012, Keir had his SAT monitor on at all times when he was at home. I wasn't in his room 24/7. (He was a teenage boy after all and Mum lurking around all the time was way uncool. This, I'm sure, he would've said to me many times if he hadn't lost his speech, so he used to tell me with a very deliberate eye roll that it was time to stop fussing and get the hell out of his room!) The monitor was the compromise – if he was getting into difficulty or was due a large cough, the machine would beep and I would go in to see if he needed suction or another bout of chest physio. The machine beeped every night around 9.30, regular as clockwork, when he had his nightly sleep apnoea. I would go in and turn him on to his side and he would sleep fairly soundly for the next few hours until it was time to once again change his position. I slept downstairs in his room for about the last two years of his life so that I could be on call. Martin offered many times, but I'm such a control freak that I couldn't allow that. I do feel rather guilty about that now, because maybe I robbed him of the ability to build up those caring skills. He accepted it with good grace and never questioned my motives.

We again managed to escape being inpatients over Christmas by the skin of our teeth (with the help of some very strong oral antibiotics and dedicated community nursing) but then the Saturday afterwards Keir's SAT monitor started beeping furiously. We ran into his room and looked at it: his SATS were fine but his heart rate was 263! I adjusted the sensor on his finger, thinking it may be a fault, but it wasn't coming down. I admit I panicked and called an ambulance for only the second time in our nine years. I was used to dealing with chest problems (the suction machine and suction catheters had become my very best friends) but a cardiac problem was completely beyond me.

The paramedic was in tears on our way to hospital as I told her a brief synopsis of Keir's story. A heart murmur had appeared from nowhere. When we arrived, Keir was taken to the high-dependency unit (HDU) and the consultant did an echocardiogram on him. We all sat in dead silence and then Erin piped up, 'Keir, it's a girl!' This made us all, including the medics, howl with laughter. Another memory created! Essentially, he was experiencing major changes in his brain function; it could no longer control his metabolism and his chemical make-up had gone haywire, causing his potassium levels to plummet.

They tried CPAP again (see Chapter 2) but he wouldn't tolerate it. I had always known that he would tell us in his own way and this he did: he had had enough. I had said to my

best friend (and constant companion during hospital stays – Dr
Donna as she became known) that I didn't think he would make
it through this time. We had a small window of opportunity
to get him home and we took it. Blue lights and sirens going,
we made it home at 1.30pm on 7 January 2014 armed with
morphine and diazepam. I had given up with his chest physio
(a thought that still haunts me today – did I do enough? Did I
give up?). He slept for the first time in a week.

Theresa and Asher

Theresa has written the most beautiful and therefore helpful
(certainly to me) words on finding acceptance, on coming to
terms with the nearly impossible idea that your child is dying.
To do that, she looked at Asher and herself in terms of 'helping
him die well'. To get there, she describes her struggle with the
huge spiritual, psychological and emotional issues – the ones
religions are created to make sense of. She starts by referring to
Ars Morendi (The Art of Dying) published in 1415, which talks
of the temptations affecting those facing death, and admits that
she herself, as the parent of a dying child, was prey to them.

> I experience lack of faith, despair, impatience, vanity and, yes,
> greed. I questioned God and felt incredibly deep despair and
> hopelessness. And impatience reared its ugly head in numerous
> forms, begging the God I thought had abandoned me to speed
> up my son's recovery to begging that same God to quicken his
> death and relieve his suffering (and, to be honest, mine, too).
> Yes, a parent really does do that. Pray their child will die.
>
> And vanity? I was so sure I could fix Asher. It was my job
> after all; I'm his mom. All I had to do was subject him to this
> test, that procedure, those surgeries. Create a hospital-like
> environment in my home. That would do it. I had the power.
>
> Worse, though, was greed. Wanting so badly for my child
> to live that I lost sight of what was important: his comfort and
> happiness.

Once Theresa had faced these demons, she was able to 'let go of the despair that prevented me doing what I could to ensure his final months were comfortable and happy'. Here she describes his final hospital admission roughly a month before he died:

> When he entered the hospital for what would be his final admission...the rubber really hit the road...we sort of had a back-pedal moment. That's when we really needed the guidance of our care team, but they had a moment of back-pedal, too, I think. Like parents, they're fixers...they're in the business of saving lives, so to counsel a family that it's time to stop must be absolutely crushing. Finally we did come to a consensus but we really had to press hard... Even after the decision was made to allow Asher to hold God's hand and find his own path, we still had moments of doubt (remember, I said it's *hard*), so we would ask for reassurance... Tell us we're making the right decision for our suffering baby...because you see how much he's hurting and how tired he is... [The team said:] 'We support whatever decision you make.' That was probably the worst thing anyone could say to us.

At this point, Theresa is desperate for their medical team to say they're doing the right thing and to take away some of the massive burden of the decision. Life is just so unfair. As parents – and you may be on your own if one parent has died or left through relationship breakdown – this is the biggest, loneliest moment. I suppose I can see that the doctors have to make *us* make the decision too because we will have doubts afterwards, and if it wasn't a joint decision, then you can involve someone else in blame, and you might. Dr Lynda Brook, a paediatric palliative consultant, was helpful to me here by explaining that the team of health professionals and family looking after a child will not all 'get it' at the same time, so 'we must find ways of sharing what we are thinking and feeling so that we can make the right decisions together when the time comes'. For her, part of the importance of the ACP is that it lays the groundwork that underpins these joint decisions, particularly when a child may no longer be able to speak.

Theresa's reaction is that this places doubt in her mind:

> What do they know that they're not telling me? Is there something we could try that wouldn't hurt him but could save him? ... Is it *us* that's tired and not him and we are being selfish?

Reading Theresa's words and having walked in those shoes, I know if you have asked yourself and made yourself answer those questions, the biggest and most painful there are, you are not being selfish: you have done the right thing by your child.

> Asher had been in the PICU for nearly three weeks. We had all come to terms that he was not going to get better and had already stopped intrusive interventions. We also knew his stay in the PICU could not be justified anymore – he wasn't receiving critical care. Our choices were to take him home, move him to the school-age unit down the hall, or try out the free-standing hospice facility.

There is no specialised children's hospice facility in Florida. Theresa describes going through the choices available:

> We knew we didn't want him to die at home. We just couldn't. We had lived for so long in a hospital and really couldn't bear the thought of being disconnected from our second family, but there are obvious space restrictions in a hospital. Although they accommodated us as much as they could, it wasn't really feasible for all of us to be in his hospital room at the same time. One of our intensivists told us that the adult hospice facility was working on accepting pediatric patients. He had a good relationship with the medical director and assured us we would be comfortable there. In addition, it was far less restrictive than the hospital could ever be (pets were allowed, anyone who wanted to could spend the night in the spacious room, etc.). We bought it.
>
> We loaded Asher in an ambulance on August 10, 2013, to check in to the hospice facility. The first night was just exhausting

but we settled in. The place was beautiful! Gorgeous landscaping, grand piano in the dining room which my daughter played for Asher. But that's about where the positives stopped. By the end of the second day, it was clear that this place was in no way prepared to care for a pediatric patient. When we had to call one of Asher's home-visiting nurses to *please* bring us his infusion pump and start IV fluids for us, we knew we were done. On the morning of the third day in the hospice facility, we called Asher's doctor and asked to be discharged to the school-age unit at the hospital. Apparently, the hospice facility wasn't too accustomed to discharging patients – especially not back to a hospital! I can't even begin to describe the red tape we had to cut through, but by 8pm on August 13, 2013, Asher was once again loaded on to an ambulance for the ride *back* to the hospital. He laughed the whole way! Seriously *laughed!* He was still giggling when we laid him in comfy, familiar hospital bed.

I'm staggered anyone would think an adult hospice would be suitable for children, given the differences between adult and paediatric palliative care. Just thinking about how an adult hospice, where most people would be elderly, and with tasteful décor and equipment appropriate to them, would appear to a child underlines how inappropriate it is. Having had some hair-raising journeys with DD, the stress of transferring a critically ill child even in an ambulance, a child with enormous medical complexity, to an environment and staff they don't know with the wrong nursing experience and then back again, just seems to me unimaginable.

Alison and Ryan

Alison, Rob and Rhys had a week with Ryan that last time in the hospice. They knew it would be the last time when they went in, unlike all their previous visits. Alison describes:

We were able to enjoy our last few days with him knowing we had all we needed on hand, health care professionals, comfort, food, quality time together with no interruptions of people knocking at the door, the telephone going, etc. Family and friends could visit and there was sibling support for Rhys.

During that time they made special memory boxes with the help of the hospice staff and moulds of Ryan's footprints to add to his fingerprints that they keep on their key rings – I'd never come across that lovely idea.[3] It was the special time that Alison had planned for the whole family.

Jane and Callum

Jane knew that this was 'always going to happen' but Callum was her 'boomerang boy' and so the decline in what proved to be the final fortnight was therefore unexpected. Normally, his health crises – a crash entailing 'blues and twos; the full works' and two days of impaired consciousness and IV antibiotics in the HDU at their local hospital – would be swiftly and happily followed by 'communicative, very cheeky chappie' Callum going home to his brother and cat. This time none of the usual medication and interventions worked and he didn't wake up. 'You could tell' this time was different, Jane recalls.

The plan was to go to their hospice, with whom they'd had an ongoing relationship for years. There was a bed available, but then everything went wrong. Somehow Jane was told that they couldn't supply enough oxygen for Callum and they had changed their rules about who they would cater for. As Jane puts it: 'That was the final straw – I was dealing with the idea that I'd be losing Callum very shortly and they were asking about dinner?!'

In the end, it worked out for the best as Jane managed to get Callum home and organised, herself, the oxygen support from the superb British Oxygen Company (BOC) who have an

---

3   There are lots of companies in the US and UK making bespoke products from fingerprints, handprints and footprints, including pendants and rings in a variety of materials including gold, silver and platinum. I've included a few in the Resources.

hour turnaround. However, Jane still doesn't understand how the communication and liaison between her team broke down, why they couldn't have bent the rules for Callum's sake, and she ended up having to sort everything out herself at the most agonising time of her life: 'He was at home, which was right as it turned out, but it could easily have been a bad outcome.'

So Jane, like me, does not want luck playing a part; she wants a better system and properly supported clinical networks.

Chapter 4

THE LAST HOURS
(24–48 HOURS ROUGHLY)

There's no away around it: this is the dying bit. Even though there's no good data on how to recognise that a child is dying, the doctors and specialist nurses *can* recognise this last couple of days. Part of the reason for this book is so parents have more information, as it is not okay for doctors to only be clear to parents that their child is going to die *now*, a few days away, when actually they knew for months it was coming. As you can imagine, if you've read this far, trying to achieve everything I've discussed in a few days flat is impossible. The result is shock, wishes don't get achieved, regrets and recriminations flow, and grief bulges. It's like having put a vast payment on your credit card without being told up front there's a huge interest payment.

You are now into living hour by hour, which then telescopes down to minute by minute at the very end. You need to call everyone you need in support as it feels *impossible* emotionally. You will get through it; you can do it, you will not let your child down because you love them.

> Dying is what happens as the body slows down in order to finally stop its work. It is the bridge between life and death. Dying is also readying the emotional self to let go. Your great gift to your child will be your calm presence...[1]

---

1   From 'Parenting a Dying Child', leaflet produced by British Columbia Children's Hospital and Canuck Place Children's Hospice, 2004.

WHAT YOU CAN DO FOR YOUR CHILD

I'll start with the very, very hardest thing first, as for me it is the key to these last hours. *Your child needs your permission to leave; to know that it's okay for them to die.* Our children will do anything to please us and not upset us, so if they think, even at a subconscious level, that trying to hold on is what you want, they will. The problem is that this invariably entails more pain and suffering *for them*. If you're fighting to keep them, this may counter the calm they need to sense not to be frightened. It's *being* with them and talking to them, loving them and keeping them comfortable. It's soft lights and favourite stories and music playing and the sound of your voices and the feel of your hands washing them and their pets purring and snoring – familiar sounds, not blue sirens and drama. It's not *doing* in a big, frenetic kind of a way.

I read this guided visualisation in the CCLG's booklet on symptom control[2] and thought it a wonderful idea to reduce stress and fear in young children. I want to quote it to give an example of something you can do if your young child is frightened:

> Try to help your child create a really rich picture of their scene. Some children may like to create a story using their favourite places or things. For example, this story is written for a child who liked the thought of flying on a magic carpet like Aladdin. These exercises are really helpful for children over the age of six. For younger children they can still benefit from little stories especially using characters from their favourite story books or TV programmes.

> - Make a picture in your mind of a flying carpet. Choose all your favourite colours to decorate it!

> - Now you can get onto your flying carpet. Perhaps you are bringing along someone for the ride, someone who makes you feel safe. You can take all your favourite things

2   Reproduced with permission from 'Managing Symptoms at Home', produced by CCLG. See 'A few publications' in the Resources.

with you on the carpet but you can pack up all your worries and pain into a case that you lock tightly with a padlock as they are not coming with you.

- Now you are ready for your trip. You can hear a whooshing sound and your carpet is rising into the air. As it rises you can feel a lovely gentle breeze on your face. Take a nice slow breath of fresh air as you rise further up. With each breath you feel more and more relaxed.

- Look down and you can see your suitcase getting further and further away from you: it feels so good. If you notice any other unpleasant feelings throw them off the magic carpet.

- The higher you go the better you feel. You can see all the villages below – look at what else you can see. Can you see the forest in the distance? If you would like to visit it take your magic carpet to wherever you want to go. You are floating down to a magical village where you see a golden lamp. This lamp is given to you. This lamp is very special and when opened, your favourite soothing colours slowly drift out making a gorgeous rainbow. You follow this rainbow – where is it taking you?

- You feel so light and calm. You are really enjoying this ride. You can go up into the clouds if you want. Just take a nice slow breath in and as you breathe slowly out your carpet rises higher and higher. You feel so light and free. You are completely relaxed and calm.

- When you are ready you can land wherever you want. Take a nice deep breath and breathe out slowly as you land.

You just keep following the child, as you have done all along. If you think they're in pain, you medicate. You don't need to try to wake them or try to feed them if they're sleeping or not hungry or thirsty; you can just keep their mouth from getting dry with a little sponge your nurse will have. You don't have to put invasive catheters in or feeding tubes. You can keep them clean and dry with incontinence pads and gentle, warm washing. Warmth comes with a favourite blanket and pets and toys. Don't worry about the visions or confusion, because your very presence as parents – your voices and smell and touch – will communicate to your darling child.

They can hear long after they have stopped responding, so talking to them quietly and stroking their hands mean they know you are there with them. Letting them know it's okay for them to die and that you'll all be okay means they know they have not failed you. What a thing for me to have to write to you. I'm four years along that road and, as my friend says, it's a long road to hoe but we are okay.

This is a quote in a recent Oxford University survey of bereaved parents:[3]

> We got to spend four hours with our baby boy... He cried, was clothed, drank some milk and gave us wonderful joy before we had to say goodbye.

WHAT TO EXPECT WHEN A BODY SHUTS DOWN

The signs do not necessarily mean death is close – you may have noticed some of these months before – but they are almost always part of dying. I have taken them from the hospice pamphlet 'Parenting a Dying Child'.[4] For some children and young people, death can come much more suddenly, just as in birth.

- Sleeps more and is difficult to waken

  I was surprised at how difficult it was to tell awake from asleep, conscious from unconscious. The lines become

---

3   National Perinatal Epidemiology Unit, 'Listening to parents after stillbirth or the death of their baby after birth', www.npeu.ox.ac.uk/listeningtoparents.

4   'Parenting a Dying Child', leaflet produced by British Columbia Children's Hospital and Canuck Place Children's Hospice, 2004.

blurred. They can yawn even when semi-conscious. Even when they appear to be awake, they may eventually stop speaking, so you assume they cannot hear, but in fact hearing is the last sense to leave. You can tell because for a while they can squeeze your hand on request when they appear to be asleep.

- Eats and drinks less and less

  The body conserves its energy and eating and digesting use it up, so part of shutting down will be not wanting/ needing to eat. Sips and spoonfuls of favourite things can continue as long as they take them, but eventually they just hold the food in their mouth and do not swallow, which is a clear sign you should stop feeding. At one point DD got constant hiccoughs, but this was probably due to some particular neurological breakdown.

- Changes to breathing patterns

  If they can no longer swallow or cough, they may take rasping breaths through an open mouth. Saliva and secretions pool at the back of their throat and this makes a distressing 'rattling' sound when they breathe known as the death rattle. There is also an abnormal pattern named Cheyne–Stokes respiration. This is a repeating cycle every couple of minutes of progressively deeper and faster breaths followed by a gradually decreasing that can end in a temporary stop called an apnoea. It does not mean your child is distressed and your health professional will be able to reassure you if you are worried about this. A final sigh can escape their lips after they have died too or if they are moved.

- The body cools

  The body very cleverly conserves most of its energy trying to keep the vital organs going as long as possible. This means that blood gets diverted away from limbs –

hands and arms, feet and then legs – and your child will feel cool and the skin may look pale and/or mottled blue.

• Less controlled bowel and bladder

The organs slowing down means that you will notice less and less urine and it will get darker. Also as death gets close, the muscles start to relax and therefore your child may lose bowel and bladder control.

• Restlessness and confusion

I found this as distressing as the breathing changes, as my maternal hormones were determined to understand this as distress and I assumed that he must need more pain relief. It's hard not to panic. They may have a fever. Your child may appear agitated and start pulling at the sheets and clothing and repeat phrases. They may not seem to know who you are or where they are or when it is – DD's dementia had clearly already caused this. Again, if in any doubt, ask the health professional with you for reassurance.

• Vision-like experiences

This, as it sounds, enters the realms of the mystical/ religious. Your child might appear to see or hear something you cannot apprehend. Their arms trace invisible tasks or meetings. Some children might appear frightened and need to be reassured. DD's dementia complicated this. One night in the last week, the Marie Curie nurse had to wake me as DD had become convinced she was burning the house down and was therefore very distressed, so I had to come and prove I was still alive.

HOW WILL YOU KNOW WHEN DEATH HAPPENS?

You may think this is a stupid thing to have to spell out, but if your child has prolonged Cheyne–Stokes breathing where they often stop and start again, as DD did for two days, it's harder to tell than you might imagine. (Again, I've copied the list from the Canadian hospice leaflet.[5])

- There is no breath or heartbeat.

- There may be a release of bowel and bladder.

- Eyes do not move even if they are open.

- Pupils are large.

- Mouth falls open as the jaw relaxes.

HOW IT WORKED FOR US AND OTHERS (THIS SECTION'S VERY HARD, SO SKIP IF NECESSARY)

We needed intensive support from our medical team for this stage, as you can imagine. My contact phone number went through to our nurse at the hospital who then contacted whoever was needed. We were incredibly fortunate that our local practice was one of the very few GP surgeries in the UK at that time with special training in end-of-life care, called the Gold Standards Framework. This meant they were completely on top of what was happening; our GP and our district nurse popped in and out constantly during the day whilst Marie Curie nurses supported us at night. The only emergency back-up we needed was for more drugs when the GP ran out of something specific and, because it was out of hours, a car ambulance sped to our local hospital pharmacy 40 minutes away to collect it and bring it to us. We were gold patients at our GP's pharmacy, which meant

---

5   'Parenting a Dying Child', leaflet produced by British Columbia Children's Hospital and Canuck Place Children's Hospice, 2004.

we were instantly prioritised and they would deliver the drugs to home – superb!

On Thursday 9 August, whilst watching a movie all together as a family on the sofa, DD had a massive seizure and clearly something catastrophic had happened neurologically. Unlike previous occasions, he did not come back after ten minutes and appeared only semi-conscious. We just kept him with us on the sofa, talking to him, and waited a good hour until the Marie Curie nurse arrived. He didn't respond to anything we said, so Toby carried him upstairs to bed. I really thought that was it, but our angel nurse shook her head and said it was not time: death was not near. So she sent us to bed to rest with the assurance that if anything changed she would wake us. (I was taking my life-saving half a lorazepam nightly, as prescribed, to ensure I slept.)

When I awoke, it was light and I rushed into his room to find him sitting up and smiling: 'Hi, Mum!' Toby and I couldn't believe it. Our nurse left as her shift had ended; by her admission, it had been a challenging night, and then the struggle began. We got him downstairs – just – but his legs were not functioning properly (pressure of tumours on his spinal nerves) and I tried to keep him occupied. It became very clear very quickly that the previous night's seizure had wiped out a huge amount of his neurological networks. He forgot everything the *instant* he was told it. His breakfast stayed in his mouth until I removed it, and asking him to take stalks off cherries resulted in him putting the stalks into his mouth – he no longer even knew what he was doing. He started to get distressed and so Toby and I decided to try to get him upstairs again and see if he needed rest. It was hopeless as I could not settle him. I called my contact number for help. These were without doubt the most difficult hours, because in all those months, when he'd been so ill, he'd never been distressed like this. I realised the seizure medication, midazolam, was my best bet; the medical team confirmed this and the oral syringe worked like a miracle. The instant it was given he was calm: 'I love it here', he said, looking out of the window into the tree tops of the little wood, and he slept. I berated myself for not having given it earlier.

When it wore off, it was obvious that it was not just seizure medication he needed. He was having lots of little seizures – *petit mals* as the nurse called them. He could no longer swallow and we needed intravenous anti-sickness medication and pain relief immediately. This is where good planning meant it was already stocked on our kitchen shelf. Our GP came out to set up the appropriate cocktail with a mini-syringe driver. This meant DD was being given a continuous topped-up dose, which could be upped if it no longer appeared to be doing its job. That was a monumental relief, but it was also shattering, because effectively it meant we knew DD would never speak to us again. I remember so well our lovely, kind doctor – a father of two himself – talking us through the decision of whether to pass a tube into DD's stomach for liquids. We all decided together it was not in DD's interest to try to keep him alive in such a dreadful state; it would have been cruel.

From that point, it was hard to tell how conscious he was; even when his eyes were open, he no longer reacted to who was present. We called my mum and sister who arrived and took over all household tasks. Rufus came in and out and would go out skateboarding with his friends in a local park for a break, whilst Holly was on play dates. Meanwhile Toby and I did three-hour shifts, only relieved by the Marie Curie nurse at night. We played DD's favourite music – particularly Pink Floyd's 'Shine on You Crazy Diamond' – we talked to him, read and kept him clean and warm. I've found a Tweet I sent that day (I was trying to raise awareness of the HeadSmart campaign and the plight of children with late-diagnosed brain tumours in the UK):

> 11 Aug: proud of my hospital corners & taught 2 change sheets with patient in the bed!

One of DD's dearest school friends came to see him. It was very calm.

By the Sunday, three days later, he had fallen into a coma and had a pronounced death rattle, which I found incredibly distressing to listen to (as I had my father's). It was helped by having him on one side with pillows propping him there, but eventually my GP decided it was worth trying a drug to relieve the symptoms; to my immense relief, it did.

He had Cheyne–Stokes breathing all Monday, his coma had become feverish and I struggled to believe a body so ravaged by cancer could keep functioning, but that shows the strength of a young person's heart. By this point he had not eaten or drunk anything since Thursday night. Holly came in to see him and I asked if she wanted to go to her friend's birthday party or stay home. I told her quite honestly that I had no idea when DD would die as he'd been in this state for days, and that if she wanted to go, DD would want her to. She knew she could come home if she wanted and she knew exactly where her mum and dad would be. She decided to go to the sleepover party. Our lovely nurse came that night and promised to wake us the second anything changed.

She awoke us all, Rufus included, at 5am, and at 6.10am on Tuesday 14 August 2012 our beloved child finally stopped breathing. The physical relief of silence after his laboured breathing, which seemed to sum up all his suffering, was instant. It was like the photo negative of a birth where the pain instantly stops and happiness flows.

Michelle and Keir

It's hard to talk about this. We knew we had brought Keir home to die but what does that mean? I had seen my grandmother dead – face fully made up in her coffin – but I had never seen anyone actually die and had no idea what to expect. Add to this that the person who is undergoing this process is the most important thing in your entire world and it gets even more complicated. I knew he had had enough and he was very, very tired but part of me hoped he would rally just one last time.

Keir more or less slept from the moment he got home. The exhaustion of a multitude of things had become too much… and he had had no sleep in hospital for the previous week. He was comfortable and restful. We kept up our vigil with many people coming and going to say goodbye.

When I woke up on the morning of Thursday 9 January 2014, two days after we had got back home, I felt there had been a change. Although he was still on his oxygen and had maintained 90(odd)% SATS on 5 litres, he was no longer able to maintain this and eventually he was back up to 15 litres to get them anything like okay. I shouted at Martin to come downstairs – it was about 8.30am. He knew in my voice that something was wrong and he woke Erin up to come down too. I rang my dad, Keir's community nurse Liz and the physio (Janice) and Hospice at Home nurse (Sue) from Derian House. They all arrived within a few minutes of each other.

We spent the morning in his room with the professionals outside in the dining room. We drank tea, laughed and watched some of Keir's favourite Disney films. Keir's breathing was becoming slower and Janice came in periodically to listen to his chest. In the final hour or so before he died, he was taking about one breath every 2–3 minutes. At this stage, we made the decision to take off his oxygen mask; it really wasn't helping him and was just keeping his heart pumping to no avail. He had slipped into unconsciousness and we knew we had to let him go.

Both of us removed the mask together, I suppose not wanting to be the one to make that last unilateral decision. We held him in our arms and told him how much we loved him and that it was okay, that he could let go. This he did. I had a moment's acute panic as he took three gasps of breath. I now know this to be just the normal dying process but I (again, unlike me) panicked that he was gasping for air and we were depriving him of life. Janice and Sue both explained very gently that this was a normal process. I just wish I had known beforehand, then it wouldn't have proved such a shock.

So Keir died at 1.10pm surrounded by all those who loved him so much. He had a good death. We couldn't save him but we could make his life full and his death calm, and this we did and that has made all the difference [and] is without doubt my greatest achievement. He was without doubt the bravest, most amazing person I will ever have the pleasure to know and I'm so proud to call him my son.

Theresa and Asher

Theresa's account of the last few days in their hospital, where they knew everyone intimately after so many years, shows just how hard it is, if you have a child who has such a complex condition, to see that one day they won't recover – they will die. She still says 'curative'…

In fact, and this is no lie, the Saturday before he died (he died on a Sunday) – so yeah, *the day before he died* – we saw some glimmer of him 'turning the corner' and actually started talking about some curative measures. He was requiring less oxygen to maintain decent saturation levels and I remember talking to one of his nurses like, 'Oh my *god* he's doing it again! What the heck with this kid? (chuckling) He just doesn't read the manual and does his own thing!' (tee hee hahhahaha – good lord.) I remember her looking at me like WTF? [and saying] 'Um, Theresa, see what happens when your body starts to straight up shut down…' Bless her for listening to me. Of course, the next day, less than 18 hours later, he died. If you go on his Facebook page you can see the posts where we joked about Asher having to go in hospital for 'tune ups'. Like every 3–4 weeks for 4–8 days at a time. Duh. Not 'tune ups', Mom. Signs.

Asher died with dignity and respect in the hospital surrounded by his family and second family. He's not tired anymore.

Alison and Ryan

Ryan sadly fell asleep in our arms on Friday 16 April 2010.
A fighter to the end, he brought joy to us every day. We're so
proud of all his achievements and to call him our son, a life that
touched so many will never be forgotten.

'It was a death fit for a king', Alison said.

Jane and Callum

I'm happy to talk about his death because it was right – if that
makes sense? Callum wasn't intubated because it would only
have been done for transfer to London for a PICU bed, if they
thought he was going to recover. Sadly it was patently obvious
that it simply wasn't going to happen this time.

He was unconscious for two weeks and never woke up. And
I'm glad because I'm 99% confident that he didn't suffer, wasn't
aware. He deserved that so much.

Still so hard knowing that the right outcome for him was
the worst for us.

Parent voice[6]

I can say quite honestly now, a few years after Megan's death
that no other experience has come close to the depth of feeling
we had as a family at the hour of Megan's death. It was as if we
all felt the same common feeling – a feeling of wonder rather
than fear. It was as if we were connected spirits. I can't describe
it. I knew then what it meant to believe in a power greater
than self.

---

6   'Being with Your Child at the End of Life's Journey: Knowing When Death Is Near
    and How to Ease the Way with Love', leaflet produced by British Columbia Children's
    Hospital and Canuck Place Children's Hospice, 2004.

Chapter 5

THE HOURS AFTER DEATH

I found this time very strange, weird even. It's as if it's not just your child that has stopped but the whole world. Then, as everything slowly starts to come into focus and restart, it jars. I felt the need to stop for ever and resented the world for not obliging.

You don't have to *do* anything. Your medical team will support you and guide you, especially if it is an unexpected death (see below). There's no rush. As I sat with DD those last four days, ideas had come to me about his Celebration (see Chapter 6) but I had not been taken through the options available for what to do in the hours and days after death, before the funeral, and we're not a religious family where there are very strong rites after death. If you're in the same situation, don't panic; it doesn't matter. Things will come to you, and you will know when you can let your child leave for the last time.

YOUR CHOICES: YOUR CHILD DOES NOT HAVE TO REMAIN WHERE THEY DIED (PoD)

Who will move your child's body and do you have to involve a funeral director?

There is *no* legal requirement to involve a funeral director in the UK and in the majority of US states (see 'Laying out and funeral arrangements and the will' in Chapter 2). If you're only reading this chapter and did not have any of these arrangements in place in advance, like me, they probably will reduce your stress levels as they have all the local contacts. For a list of accredited ones

in the UK, see the National Association of Funeral Directors (see
Resources). They will organise absolutely everything including
the ceremony/service if you wish them to. The Natural Death
Centre in the UK also has a list of funeral directors who are
especially flexible in terms of you being able to choose for them
to only do certain things. In other words, you can use a funeral
director as much or as little as you wish.

In the US, there are very strong non-profit organisations
advising the public on their legal rights and how to get the most
cost-effective service. Access the Funeral Consumers Alliance
(FCA) website to find your local group (see Resources for details).

Getting your child's body out of the hospital

Funeral directors will be able to speed up the process of moving
your child's body; however, health professionals are aware, or
should be, that, for some families, doing it themselves is very
important, and if the family has planned this, it should not take
any longer. This is also the case in the US but families need
the required permits to do so. In order to understand how the
process works for getting your child's body out of hospital, I've
visited the mortuary service at Southampton General Hospital.
This is run by incredibly helpful and kind technicians and has a
good out-of-hours service, but all hospitals are different – some
are run by porters, some do not operate out of hours. NICU and
PICU units have their own service and policies if it is a stillbirth
or neonatal death.

I realised I had big preconceptions about what a mortuary
was, based on the stigma surrounding the idea of it. Before I had
visited, I thought I would not have liked DD to go there had he
died in hospital, but I've totally changed my mind. Their entire
ethos is based on continuity of care – I hadn't thought about
that. The public are not permitted in the actual mortuary; they
have a relative's room and a viewing room. I thought the viewing
room would be cold and dark, but in reality it's a bright, softly
lit room with soft furnishings and calm pictures to try to ease

the pain for families. I realise I had it confused in my head with the metal trolleys of pathology, a totally different department. Southampton's is totally private and I didn't get any sense of 'viewing' from the outside that you see in TV dramas.

Usually after about a couple of hours (for babies, see next paragraph), the child's body will be moved from the ward down to the mortuary viewing room. Parents can accompany them or meet them there with the nursing staff or bereavement team in support. If you accompany them, it's recommended to have the child on their hospital bed rather than trying to carry them (unless it is a baby) in case you slipped and fell: people in the corridors just assume they're asleep post-operation. You can stay there with your child and nursing staff in support whilst the necessary paperwork is completed. Some hospitals have facilities as part of their chapel of rest where a body can be laid out; in Southampton, you can lay out your child and look after them in the viewing room whilst you wait for transport arrangements to be made, but hospitals all differ, so you need to check. Generally speaking, you will be looked after by the staff on the ward on which your child died, but for older teens and young people the hospital bereavement service will support you in whatever choice you make.

In the case of babies who have died, most families in the UK are able to stay with their baby, together as a couple, away from other babies and their families in the hospital for as long as they need. On average, after a neonatal death a family will spend two days, and after a stillbirth, one, in the hospital being supported by the team. This gives time for families to hold and care for their baby, make precious memories, get advice on how to deal with milk production, get a counselling referral and information on funerals. The unit should have accurately informed the mother's GP and community midwife within one working day of the death, so there is support after discharge.

In the UK, as long as the death has been certified, your child's body can be released by the mortuary to you – you do *not* need the 'green form' (see Chapter 6).

Moving a body yourself

There is *no* legal requirement in the UK or the majority of US states (see 'Laying out and funeral arrangements and the will' in Chapter 2) to use a hearse and funeral director. It can be any vehicle into which you can slide a body from a hospital trolley. Parking your car at the back of the hospital mortuary means you will have privacy and plenty of help doing this. The mortuary team advised me that they are only happy to release a body once the family has something firm for the body to rest on so that it is safe in transit – a stretcher (some funeral directors will lend you one) or a coffin or a wicker basket or the Respect Everybody Shroud (see Chapter 6). This again emphasises that you need to have done some planning in advance if you're not using a funeral director as it will take time to deliver one of these to the mortuary. If you are not using a funeral director but want a coffin, you can buy direct from certain suppliers listed on the website at the Natural Death Centre in the UK; the FCA also has information on this in the US (see Resources).

Given our physical and emotional state as bereaved parents, it's a good idea to nominate a driver unless you feel very strongly that you want to drive. However, it is advisable to notify the police you are moving a body from hospital/home/hospice, just in case you get stopped for a traffic infringement; otherwise, you'll have some explaining to do! If you prefer, the mortuary staff and bereavement team can give you a written letter explaining to the police the situation and they can also ring them for you. In Scotland, they will automatically do this if it is a baby being transported home by the parents. In the UK, you are *not* required to have the actual death certificate in the car – it only matters that the death has been certified – but in the US you *do*. If the death has not yet been certified and you want to move the body in the UK, you will need permission from the coroner or procurator fiscal (Scotland). You will also need permission from them if you wish to cross the border into Northern Ireland, the Isle of Man, Channel Isles or Scotland, or to take the body abroad, but ask your team as some UK coroners do like families to seek permission before moving their child. It is perfectly legal to cross county borders in England and Wales and there is no charge to so. Anyone who tells you otherwise is incorrect.

In the US, most states require a Disposition Permit or Burial Transit Permit. Contact the state or local Department of Health Bureau of Vital Statistics for details.

Where to lay out your child's body until the funeral/celebration

AT HOME

There's no place like home! However, you will need to cool the body to keep it in good condition (see the 'Changes to the body' section below). You will need to turn the heating off in the room and also keep windows shut in summer months to prevent flies coming inside, as they are naturally attracted to a body, but conversely open the windows in the depths of winter to help keep the body cool (see Michelle's story below). Be aware that you will need to control the number of people coming into the room at the same time, as they will raise the temperature of the room significantly. NHS guidance is that cooling of the body should start within 2–4 hours.

Nearly all major hospitals and hospices have available a portable mini-cooling system. These usually consist of a small unit which circulates fluid through the cooling pad that is laid either on top of the body or underneath (depending on the type and size of the unit) via a slim hose – a sort of electric duvet that chills rather than warms. There are various sizes, including one suitable for children up to adult, and the CuddleCot is designed specifically for babies (including the premature). You can ask to be lent a unit by your hospice (hospitals can't spare them) to have at home; you'll need purified/deionised still water (available from any garage), not tap water, and an electrical socket nearby. At 11kg, the Covercool mini system is small enough to carry upstairs. There are also small refrigeration units being manufactured by other companies for this purpose, which your hospice may have as an alternative (see Resources). Even with this in place, best current advice is to aim for a burial/cremation within five days. Parents who have kept their child for more than two weeks find that environmental health and social services can become involved. In the US, the NHFA has a really useful *Quick Guide* to the legal requirements in your state.[1]

Families have hired portable air-conditioning units to help cool a room down in the summer, but after long discussions with technicians at various companies it's clear this can't keep a room below 16°C/60°F which is too warm to stop a body deteriorating even with plenty of disposable icepacks, whereas the Covercool can keep the body at 8–10°C/46–50°F. Southampton's mortuary technicians advised that if you cannot borrow a Covercool or refrigeration and it is absolutely necessary to keep the body longer than a couple of days – maybe you're waiting for a relative to arrive from abroad or you cannot get an earlier funeral slot – embalming will keep the body in good condition for longer but be aware this will often then prevent you being able to have a natural burial (see Chapter 6).

AT YOUR LOCAL HOSPICE

Their special end-of-life care suite incorporates a unit to keep the room cool after death. You can go and be with your child there any time 24/7 with the family until the funeral. There is no legal limit on the length of stay, but again the whole family should be aware of changes to the body during this time. Several families I know stayed a week at their hospice at this time.

AT THE FUNERAL DIRECTOR'S

You simply need to make an appointment to see your child's body and they will go to great lengths to accommodate you, given the circumstances. There is no legal requirement for your child's body to be embalmed if you want to view your child's body at the funeral directors. Embalming is *not* necessary

---

1   See http://homefuneralalliance.org/wp-content/uploads/2016/01/Quick-Guide-to-Home-Funerals-By-State.pdf.

or required for children and young people unless advised by the funeral director or requested by the family on religious or practical grounds. Similarly in the US, embalming is not required if the burial is taking place within 24 hours after death but most states accept refrigeration as a viable alternative – again, see the NHFA pdf *Quick Guide* for the legal requirements in your state. Embalming is a process whereby chemicals are introduced into your child's body to stop deterioration and it is has to be done at a funeral director's premises or at your local mortuary with your permission. It can affect whether you can have a natural burial (see Chapter 6). Unfortunately, at the moment some health professionals are wrongly advising families that they *have to* embalm their child after death.

WHAT CAN YOU DO FOR YOUR CHILD AFTER THEY HAVE DIED?

In no particular order:

- Change the bedding to something particularly lovely.

- Put flowers in the room and candles/incense.

- Play music.

- Get into bed with your child for a cuddle.

- Talk to your child and take care of them as you always have done.

- Remove any tubing or intravenous lines (unless the death is unexpected – see below) and get rid of all medical equipment in the room.

- Wash them, brush their hair, then dress them in a chosen outfit.

- Favourite toys and pictures can be brought in, if they weren't already there – especially a board of special pictures, words and photographs.

- Move more chairs into the room so family and friends can come and sit with you if you wish and pay their respects to your child. Be aware that this increases the temperature in the room, and if you do not have a Covercool or refrigeration, you may need to cool the body to keep it in good condition. Disposable ice-packs covered with a cloth, to prevent damage to your child's skin, are useful for this.

- Discuss the funeral and celebration details, including nominating someone to contact people about your child's death, especially their friends. There is endless marvellous help online, including help writing a eulogy.

- Help the siblings understand what has happened and is going to happen. If they were not present at the death, seeing the body is a way for them to understand that death is final and that their sibling is not suffering any more. They can react in a huge variety of ways from loud anger through to silent nothing and everything in between, something well described in CCLG's booklet.[2] Making memory boxes containing special things that will bring back lovely memories of their dead sibling can be very helpful if you have not started the process already.

- Keep a lock of their hair and/or take a handprint.

- Decorate the casket/coffin/box or choose a vessel for the ashes. You could make your own shroud or coffin.

- Place your child in their coffin/casket or in a shroud (any kind of fabric covering). There is *no* legal requirement in the US or UK to have a body in a coffin/casket. UK law only asks that a body be covered *in public* – not to do so would 'outrage public decency'.

- Say goodbye.

---

2   CCLG (2015) *Facing the Death of Your Child: Suggestions and Help for Families, Before and Afterwards* (see Resources for details).

CHANGES TO THE BODY

(Please read this if you want to keep your child's body at home or at the hospice before the funeral. If you can't stand the idea of thinking about this, skip it and organise for the funeral director to come and collect the body as soon as possible. If you cannot bear the idea of this breakdown of their body or your religion requires it, you can ask the undertaker to embalm their body, which is a process that will temporarily preserve it. NB. The death must be registered (see below) before embalming is allowed to proceed.)

The cessation of life is known as *somatic death*, and immediately following this the process called *molecular death* begins, as cells begin to die without the circulation of oxygen from the heart. In warm weather, clearly this will happen faster. If you are going to look after the body yourself rather than hand your child over immediately to an undertaker, you need to be aware of these signs so they are not a shock and you can warn siblings and visitors. The more you move a body, the quicker it deteriorates, and if your child has undergone a lot of treatment, such as chemotherapy, during their illness or if they have received a lot of intensive medical interventions at the very end of their life, this can also affect the condition of their body after death. All this means that it is very difficult to say how long it takes for any of these changes to take place. For this reason, the Natural Death Centre advises that you leave it no longer than five days from death to the burial or cremation if you have a body at home or in a cool room at the hospice, but there is in fact no legal requirement on the length of time in the UK.

Algor mortis – the death chill. As soon as the heart stops beating, the body immediately starts to cool down. This process of cooling can take from two to eight hours.

Livor mortis – also known as lividity. This is the dark purple colouring that comes from the pooling of blood in the veins and capillary beds after the blood has stopped pumping around the body. It can make quite big patches, which become fixed after about 10–12 hours. It's most noticeable in the earlobes and fingernail beds, but also where the child's body is in contact with an underlying surface.

Rigor mortis – the one we all hear on the TV crime series. There's a short period after death where the muscles are floppy, which makes the body easy to move, but then usually within 3–4 hours the muscles stiffen, which is known as rigor mortis. It disappears 36–48 hours after death. You need to know about this if you wish to dress your own child in favourite clothes, which I did.

Eye changes. If you do not shut the child's eyes at death – our district nurse shut DD's – they cannot later be naturally closed. If you wish the eyes to be closed later, you need to ask the undertaker to do it. The eyes may gain a sunken appearance.

Pallor and skin dryness. Paleness comes from the lack of blood circulating. The skin can also become dry for the same reason, so you can moisturise their lips if you wish with Vaseline or a favourite lip balm.

Bleeding. The only way to stop this if it occurs is to physically block the flow. Using dark towels will make it less obvious. If it becomes a problem, you can get your nurse to contact the undertaker for you.

Fluids. There's no way to be delicate about this; like birth's aftermath, death is messy and then eventually smelly. I remember so well my district nurse helping me with DD and warning me as we moved his body that it would probably leak very unpleasant/shocking looking fluid. It did and it reminded me of the shock of seeing my babies' meconium post-partum and being glad I'd been warned! We had put pads under him and had plenty of towels and wipes to hand.

NB. Also you will not be allowed to wash/move/remove intravenous lines or tubes or transfer your child to a cool room if the death was unexpected, until the medical practitioner arrives. You would certainly need to check with the Medical Examiner for your state in the US too.

THE LEGAL PAPERWORK STUFF

I have no memory of this. My darling sister and our medical team did most of it. I'm going to whizz through it as quickly as I can, mostly using the resource for professionals produced by Together for Short Lives (see 'A few publications' in the Resources).

Expected death is the natural and inevitable end to an irreversible terminal illness. This was the category DD fell into.

Unexpected death[3]

I have to include this to prepare any parents of a child with a life-limiting or life-threatening condition, so they are not alarmed or shocked if it happens to their family. It sounds bizarre that a death could be 'unexpected' when your child has a condition that means they will at some point die prematurely. It happens fairly often in the UK because the child is usually looked after by a team of specialists at a large hospital and not by the GP locally. This means that if you're at home and your child's health suddenly deteriorates and they die, it will be unexpected if the GP was not warned.[4] Unexpected death is defined in the UK as such if it is sudden and unforeseen. In the context of a baby, child or young person with a life-threatening or life-limiting condition, it does not mean the death was suspicious. A death is unexpected if:

---

3   There is good information on the process of what happens in the Lullaby Trust Child Death Review booklet, www.lullabytrust.org.uk/bereavement-support/child-death-review-process.

4   See 'How to reduce the chance of an unexpected death' in Chapter 2.

- it was not anticipated as a significant possibility, 24 hours before the death

- there was a similarly unexpected collapse leading to or precipitating the events leading to the death

- the child had not been seen by the certifying doctor within the last 14 days of life

- death occurred within 24 hours of admission to hospital or during surgery/recovering from anaesthetics.

UK national and local policies then have their own procedures to follow. The doctor has to inform the coroner (England and Wales) or procurator fiscal (Scotland). If the doctor and coroner agree on the cause of death, then the Medical Certification of Cause of Death (MCCD) can be completed. If there are any concerns at all, by anyone – the coroner, health professionals or the parents themselves – a post-mortem (PM) may be ordered. A PM is a legal requirement for any sudden death when the cause is not apparent and is always necessary after a post-operative death or death within 24 hours of hospital admission. If a PM is ordered, families have no legal right to refuse and it would go ahead with or without their consent.[5] The burial or cremation will not be able to take place until this has happened and it can affect being able to have your child's body at home after death. If you choose not to have a post-mortem, if one is offered, be aware that it would be very difficult to be granted an inquest later. If you wish to donate your child's brain to research, arrangements would have to be put in place for the brain to be retrieved (see section 'Organ/tissue donation and body donation (including brain)' in Chapter 2).

It would be unusual for the coroner to order a post-mortem in the case of a child with a life-shortening condition, but it does happen as the cause of death is not necessarily the disease. For example, it could be an infection that causes the death, to which

---

5   For Northern Ireland, consult www.coronersni.gov.uk.

the child's disease made them vulnerable. Most parents who lose a baby are asked to consent to a post-mortem and most reported that they felt informed enough about the process.[6] Post-mortems can often be helpful – for example, to help parents consider the implications of future pregnancies, to help answer questions about the death, or if parents wish it to provide information that will assist research into rare childhood conditions. Currently, it is taking over two months to receive the results of a baby's post-mortem for more than half the parents in a recent study[7] and nearly all met with their consultant at least once after their babies' death to discuss it. Most parents are given a cause of death for their baby, prematurity being the most common cause in neonates; where a cause was able to be identified in stillbirths, it was most commonly placental problems.

NB. Stillbirths[8] are not currently reported to the coroner and even after a PM has been carried out, more than a quarter were described as 'unexplained'.[9]

If the case proceeds to a full inquest, the coroner will sign the death certificate after the PM plus any certificates necessary for burial or cremation, and the child's body will be officially released to the parents (except in the most exceptional circumstances).

The US system is not dissimilar but there are different protocols to adhere to according to state laws. If the death was sudden, even if from natural causes, it is the Medical Examiner or Coroner who fills in the Cause of Death rather than the attending doctor. However in Pierce County, Washington State, if parents call in to report their child has died at home of their disease, families are told by the on-call doctor at their major hospital that they have to call 911; they have no choice and that automatically brings the police, coroner and paramedics to attend. Worse, the latter are legally required to perform CPR.

---

6   National Perinatal Epidemiology Unit, University of Oxford, 'Listening to parents after stillbirth or the death of their baby after birth', www.npeu.ox.ac.uk/listeningtoparents.

7   'Listening to parents after stillbirth or the death of their baby after birth' (see note 6).

8   Stillbirthstories.org is a resource where bereaved parents can listen to other parents who have been through the experience to help them understand how decisions were made.

9   'Listening to parents after stillbirth or the death of their baby after birth' (see note 6).

One family there I spoke to, whose four-year-old had been on palliative support for a month previously and then died from their brain tumour at home, had to watch paramedics hook up and then perform CPR on their child who had been dead at this point for *four hours*. If I went into shock being told this story, you can imagine the impact on the family. The same has happened elsewhere in the US. If this awful story doesn't tell you the system needs to be reformed immediately in the US, with proper linked specialist children's palliative care everywhere and not just in a few major cities, nothing will. Proper linked care would have meant someone would have taken the family through what happens after death and enabled them to have a signed DNR/POLST for their child to prevent just this sort of intervention.

Verification of death (UK)

This is the procedure for stating when a patient has actually died – the physiological assessment to confirm the fact of death. In the UK, a nurse or a paramedic can do this.[10] Whoever verifies it has to check: there is no radial pulse; no carotid pulse; no effort to breathe – no sounds in a stethoscope for one minute; no eye movements – the pupils must be fixed and dilated and not react to light; and no response to painful stimuli. This must be recorded in the care record or medical notes and include the place, date and time of death, who was present, and the fact that death was verified. The medical practitioner who will provide the MCCD will be given written notification as soon as possible.

It is only following this process that any parenteral drug administration can be stopped and equipment removed with parental consent. Controlled drugs present must be recorded and

---

10 Together for Short Lives has an excellent booklet on this process for health professionals but especially children's nurses, entitled 'The verification of expected death in childhood: Guidance for children's palliative care services'. It is available at www.togetherforshortlives.org.uk/assets/0000/1856/FINAL_TfSL_Verification_of_Expected_Death_in_Childhood_Report.pdf.

the drugs retained (and disposed of) according to regulation and policy.

Certification of death[11]

You cannot register a death if this certification has not been done first, and by law the cause of death has to be established by a medical practitioner – either the one who has been treating the child or the one who saw them last. In DD's case, this was our GP as his oncologist works in Southampton General Hospital and hadn't seen him for the last three months. The certifying doctor has to complete a MCCD which includes a statement of the cause of death, the date the child died, the date the child was last seen alive and whether they have seen the body after death. The correct wording and recording of a death is incredibly important to families, not only for themselves but also in terms of informing future policy or treatments, especially if it would prevent similar deaths.

In the US, if the death is from natural causes, the cause of death section will typically be filled in by the physician who cared for the child and knew their medical history. They will give the date, time and cause of death.

Notification of death (UK)

This is required within 24 hours for *all* deaths in under-18s, including babies, to the appropriate inspectorate. This includes the Local Safeguarding Children Board (LSCB) which is required to review all child deaths via the Child Death Overview Panel (CDOP).[12] Your doctor will do this. This information gives the

11 The UK government is in the midst of changing this process. The role of a medical examiner will be introduced. Essentially, the cause of all deaths that do not need to be investigated by a coroner would then be confirmed by a medical examiner before a medical certificate of cause of death is issued. One of the aims is to be able to speed up the process of getting a child's body out of hospital to minimise distress to parents.

12 See the Lullaby Trust Child Death Review booklet, www.lullabytrust.org.uk/bereavement-support/child-death-review-process.

data and evidence needed to underpin and inform national policies in the area of children and young people's health in order to prevent future deaths.

Registration of death

All deaths have to be registered by appointment in England and Wales within five days in the district where they have died or where they lived (within eight days in Scotland); only then is a funeral/celebration allowed to take place. Close family members can register the death – my sister did for us – or someone who was present. The actual death certificate is the entry in the death register; the registrar issues certified, signed copies of this entry.

The best place to check for everything official that needs to be done after the death is www.direct.gov.uk/en/ Governmentcitizensandrights/Death/WhatToDoAfterADeath/ Guide/index.htm.

Tragically, if your baby has died, even one born premature after 24 weeks, you will need to register the birth as well. This is not necessarily the case in the US where often a 'certificate of birth resulting in stillbirth' is issued.

Ireland, Northern Ireland and Scotland all have slightly varying rules, so check their local government websites under 'register a death'.

In the US, most states again allow family members to file the US Standard Certificate of Death and state law lays down the number of days in which this must be done. If you need help, contact the registrar at your state's Department of Health Bureau of Vital Statistics. It is often possible to file and receive a copy the same day, but you should be prepared to pay a small fee for each copy. Most states also allow online order of the certificate via a government-authorised service at VitalChek. Funeral directors will do it for you if you wish.

HOW IT WORKED FOR US AND OTHERS

I felt unanchored, unmoored. The finality of that last breath, the absence, floored me. I can't speak for my husband. My reaction was to be sort of stupefied, numb and passive until suddenly I would be violently seized by something I had decided needed to happen *now* and galvanised into frantic activity. Mid-afternoon of the day DD died, for example, I suddenly decided that I never wanted to see any medical equipment associated with his illness in my house ever again and went tearing around throwing away bin-loads of drugs, tubes, lines and pads. I had cried more than my body weight in tears those four days sitting with him in a coma, but after he died, after the first few hours, I was dry. Spent.

Our GP and district nurse (DN) came around 8am and verified and certified the death and then our extraordinary Marie Curie nurse left. I still can't believe that we had the luck to have a nurse with experience in both elderly Alzheimer's patients and children who turned out also to be a bereaved parent – her name is graffitied on my heart. The DN closed his eyes and stayed with us as I talked through what we were going to do. Holly was driven back from her sleepover with friends and arrived at around 9am and we took her upstairs to see her adored brother. I feel that if you don't actually see a body, it's harder to take in and believe that they are dead. She seemed too shocked to react but she looked and listened.

I was determined that both she and Rufus understood that they would never be expected to replace their brother in any conceivable way; DD would want them to fulfil their own dreams, not try to carry out his. I was equally determined they would not feel guilty if they were relieved their brother had died; I told them that was a completely natural and normal reaction because his illness had been horrendous in so many ways and it had gone on so long, making their brother suffer. I told them I was very proud of them and that we were incredibly lucky to have had a son and brother to lose; we knew children who had longed for a sibling and never been granted that wish.

Never were the poet Alfred, Lord Tennyson's lines more apt: 'Tis better to have loved and lost / Than never to have loved at all.'

Someone rang our Buddhist friend who lived locally. He came straight over, lit incense sticks in DD's room and sat, meditated and prayed with his body. We knew DD would have loved that.

I didn't want to get into bed with DD or cuddle him as I had been doing that all along. Now that he was no longer there, that was how I felt; I didn't want his body in the house but I *did* want to take care of him before he finally left. I wanted to wash his body with our nurse and dress him in clothes Toby, Rufus, Holly and I had chosen together. So, before rigor mortis had set in, I undressed, bathed and clothed DD with the help of our nurse and it remains a very special memory. It's also why I treasure my continued contact with this nurse through her child at our primary school. Taking care of him like this felt absolutely right and I completely understand why it's a fundamental part of many religious practices associated with death. I loathed the idea of an undertaker touching him at all – he didn't know my child. I know this is partly because 16 years before I had taken against seeing their black-clothed figures take my father away in silence in a black bag and I didn't like it. I don't like black in the context of death, I hate plastic bags (so did DD on environmental grounds) and silence is not a quality much associated with our family! When the undertaker had said all those years ago, voice lowered, that Dad was being taken to a chapel of rest, my sister famously retorted, 'He doesn't like resting. He likes to party!'

How I wish I had known that Toby and I needn't have involved an undertaker at all. We could have got a cooling system from our local hospice and kept his body at home for the couple of days before we could get a slot at the crematorium. We then could have quite legally driven his body straight to the crematorium ourselves and then brought his ashes back home afterwards for his Celebration, but we were wrongly told it was *illegal* to cross county lines with a body. Even being told I couldn't, I nearly did anyway in a mood of furious let-them-try-and-stop-a-bereaved-mother! However, I was so exhausted and I realised it wasn't a fight I could face at that moment. How I hope to prevent another parent giving in at a time when it matters so much! So our local undertaker collected him the day that he died and they were lovely about everything. We wrapped DD in a simple sheet – I couldn't even entertain the thought of him shut in a coffin – and he was carried downstairs and outside to their car and driven away for the last time. That was a pain that will never be described except by a primal howl.

Whilst Rufus went to bed to catch up on sleep, having been up half the night with us, Holly then spent hours with a close family friend decorating a box for the ashes to be kept in (see the cover of this book!). It was gorgeous and important, and Toby and I hoped it made her feel really involved with all the decisions we were making as a family for her brother. Toby had also made a lovely series of wonderful pictures of DD, which scrolled through automatically in a wooden photo frame for her bedroom.

All DD's friends met up outside their school the night after he died and lit candles together and placed flowers at an impromptu shrine. They were there for hours telling stories about him. I simply couldn't bear the weight that night and physically could not go, but I loved that they all met up to remember him. They still post messages on Facebook on his deathday and continue to raise awareness of brain tumour symptoms with the HeadSmart campaign, which really gives me strength. I'm so proud of them all.

Writing this, I understand that our family's planning was very good for *before* the death but there was nothing in place for *afterwards*, and of course you are so exhausted and in pain from grief that you end up going along with things that your health professionals know about. If I'd known what I know now, we would have planned this differently and then our family and community would have carried it out for and with us.

Theresa and Asher

Theresa is the only mum in this book whose child died in hospital. I was most concerned that parents would get time with their child's body, which is effectively unlimited at home and in a hospice, and Theresa reassured me:

> They were amazing at letting us have all the time we needed with Asher's body. My dear friend (a PICU nurse) helped me bathe him and wash his incredible hair. Another friend (nurse) took the responsibility of carrying Asher to the morgue and ensured he was appropriately cared for.

However, when she was checking my section on reasons why you might not want to die in hospital (Chapter 2), she also acknowledged that it was 'weird':

> I mean, strangers are walking around with their kids and here you sit in silent darkness with your child's dead body. I mean at some point you have to open the door to let visitors in or take a breath yourself and who doesn't walk by an open hospital door and look – it's just habit. I can't imagine what those families who saw what was happening in Asher's room thought. We were numb so I didn't really think about it at the time, but now it must have been a cold dose of reality to some of those parents. Like a punch straight to the gut.

Michelle and Keir

> Immediately after Keir died, Erin had a huge panic attack. It is the first time that had happened to her. I had been lying next to him on the bed as he died and she now wanted to lie with him and give him a cuddle. As soon as she changed places with me, the enormity of what had happened hit her like a train. Keir's lips had already started to change colour and she was really freaked out by it. As she said, she didn't want to remember him like that. She seldom went into his room in the week that he

was with us before his funeral – she could handle him dying, but not being reminded of it time after time.

I think we all felt a huge sense of relief the moments after he died. I appreciate this is an alien concept – after all, we had just lost our child – but the relief was palpable. Relief for him that he didn't have to soldier on bravely in discomfort and pain, being continually reliant on oxygen therapy and not being able to have any kind of quality of life. There was also relief for ourselves; we had spent nine years in a state of intense stress and abject misery (not on the surface, sometimes we enjoyed life – usually when Keir was laughing – but you cannot underestimate the daily agony of watching your child slip away incrementally before your very eyes). This kind of pain takes its toll on you. You hold it together while it's going on, but when it's over, that's when you start to unravel either physically, mentally or both. The day after Keir died, I was mopping my floor and a thought suddenly struck me: what would people think if they saw me doing this? They would think, her child's just died and she's mopping her floors – is she absolutely bat-shit crazy? I also thought why am I bothering to do this? What is the point – not just of this, but of anything? One of my two main reasons for living was now gone and with him my sense of purpose.

This relief was extremely short-lived. The numbness gives way to agony and distress the like of which I would not wish on the very worst of us.

We kept Keir at home between his death and the funeral. It was early January and fiercely cold outside. The funeral director who visited us the day after he died had told us that it would be fine for us to keep him with us. To be honest, I don't think I could have borne it if he had been taken at that point. I needed that time to gather my somewhat irrational thoughts. When the second doctor came to certify death (for the purposes of cremation), I actually asked him if Keir was really dead. He looked at me with a mixture of pity and incredulity – after all it was two days after he had died – but I had to check. In fact, thinking about it, I think I asked that question on more than one occasion.

So we turned the radiator off in his room and made sure all the windows were closed, we closed the blinds for privacy (even though his room was not overlooked) – it just seemed the right thing to do. The light still shone on him, especially his face, and he looked peaceful and at rest. We had closed his eyes and turned him on to his back straight after he died to avoid the inevitable pooling and purple marking that follows after. He was still my beautiful boy and my instinct was to keep him warm but he was so cold. I found that part really distressing. We had washed him and dressed him in some new clothes that we had got him for Christmas and he looked grown-up and tiny all at the same time. I covered him with a thin blanket to fool my mind into thinking he was cosy, but the room was freezing. I love candles and I lit one in his room that burned for the full week between death and his funeral – I bought the same candle after he was gone from us and one tiny waft of the scent transports me back to that time and place. Smell is such an important part of memory and should not be underestimated.

Let me tell you about the light that shone on Keir after he died. One of his regular health care workers was a lovely young woman who was a practising Muslim. I am not religious at all but something she said struck me and I found comfort in it. When she came to see him after he had died (she had been there minutes after his death but there was so much happening, she wanted to come back in a moment of peace), she said, 'He has so much light in his face.' I said, 'Yes, the light shines through the blinds and hits his face.' She said, 'No, in Islam we call it Noor. It is light that comes from within and shines out.' That just about sums Keir up.

Back to practicalities: we had a Statement of Intent for Keir. Our GP issued it the day we brought him home from hospital. This enabled us to have little involvement with HM Coroner… Because Keir had a SOI, the Senior Coroner in our jurisdiction was satisfied to accept the cause of death as given by our GP and happy for him to issue the MCCD. At this point I have to give a big shout-out to our amazing GP practice yet again – the GP that came out to issue the SOI was also a practising Muslim. He issued the document on the Tuesday that we brought Keir home and told us that he didn't work on Fridays but should anything happen on Friday, to ring him on his mobile and he would attend...

I read a poem I found after Keir died. I don't know who it's written by but I found these lines so very apt:

So when I saw you sleeping
So peaceful, free from pain
I could not wish you back
To suffer that again.[13]

Alison and Ryan

As Alison had been able to plan for this before Ryan died, she says it meant that she could just focus on being with him and the family instead of being stressed in her distress by funeral arrangements and then going along with something that was not right. She describes how:

After Ryan had died, the hospice has an end-of-life suite and once your child as passed away they are taken to the 'Snowflake Room' (special cold bedroom). This allows your child to remain at the hospice after their passing, enabling you to leave your child in a safe and familiar environment with the access to spend time saying goodbye in an informal and supportive environment. We stayed with Ryan for the weekend after his passing and, whilst leaving him in Snowflake was the hardest thing we have ever done, we still had peace of mind that at a time that he could not be with us he was still in the peace, comfort and security of familiar surroundings.

---

13   It's from a poem called 'God saw you getting tired' by Frances and Kathleen Coelho.

Jane and Callum

I could not believe how you are immediately alone after your child's death and everything is being stripped away.

The best way to explain it is in a before and after scenario really...

BEFORE
Callum went to school, had outpatient appointments, physio, OT, Saturday club, speech and language therapy (SALT), hospital admissions, hospice respite breaks. I went to meetings with assorted people such as the school nurse, school team, speciality doctors and nurses, made phone calls, sent emails and was in constant contact with people. Then there were others like the supplies delivery driver, wheelchair services technician and the hoist service engineers.

AFTER
Without Callum, there was no need for any of the above to be involved with us anymore – and other children needed them. So at the same time as losing Callum, my support network, who felt almost like friends and family, vanished too. A week to the day after he died it was Callum's birthday and we still held a party. The ceiling track hoist in his bedroom was taken down the same day. His wheelchair-accessible van was taken back by Motability. Connor had to leave Young Carers and the friends he made there. He was fortunate in being allowed to return for a final session to say goodbye. As a rule, it just stops. Whilst I understand that there is a massively oversubscribed waiting list, it was beyond harsh.

Jane and I call this the abyss-void.

Chapter 6

CELEBRATION

Celebration – I have deliberately chosen this word instead of 'funeral' or 'memorial' because it's my favourite. To celebrate a life that is completed. More than that, it was a word to show I intended from the start to aim for the point where I would be able to access memories of DD and they would make me happy, instead of just causing infinite pain. I know some people completely disagree about using celebration in the context of death. It's your choice.

The word 'funeral' comes from the Latin word *funus*, meaning death rites, which encompass not just the ceremony but also the death, the corpse, funeral procession and burial rites. If you are from a religious background, you will have clear and probably ancient ceremonies to follow, but if, like my family, you are not, you are free to create your very own bespoke ceremony – DIY! There are no rules. There is no requirement, for example, that says a vicar or someone religious has to be present – it's up to you. The law in the UK merely states that after death a body must either be cremated or buried, but the details and timing of the accompanying ceremonies are entirely up to families. The wonders of a 21st-century online world open up a kaleidoscope of ideas, services and products to choose from, including international remembrance services for people who have lost a child at any stage of pregnancy, birth or in infancy.[1] You can have a service anywhere meaningful to your family.

---

1   See, for example, www.sayinggooddbye.org/services. Also, www.childofmine.org.uk has some lovely ideas, links and support on their website.

First, you will need:

- A Certificate for Burial or Cremation from the registrar of births/deaths or coroner *before* the burial/cremation takes place (the green form; in Northern Ireland it is known as form GRO 21 and it is form 14 in Scotland). You need to give this to your funeral director in order for the burial or cremation to take place or get the slip at the bottom back to the registrar after your ceremony if you're doing it yourself (see below).

  In the US, you will need to check the requirements for your state.

BURIAL (INTERMENT)

Your child can be buried in a churchyard – in theory, anyone living in a parish in the UK has the right to be buried next to relatives in the parish churchyard, but in practice many are full – a local authority cemetery, a private cemetery or on private land. Each cemetery will have its own regulations and directions and you just need to contact them. Unfortunately, burials are often very expensive and only some of these costs may be waived for children and young people.[2]

Natural burial sites

If you are someone with concerns about the environment, this might present a good option. There are now hundreds of these sites all over the UK used by the community, and the land is managed to enhance wildlife habitats and encourage biodiversity. The Natural Death Centre recommends that you use one that is a member of the Association of Natural Burial Grounds (ANBG) and has links on its website (see 'Useful contacts' in the

---

2   The Welsh Government has announced it would abolish burial fees for children. More pressure needs to be brought to bear to ensure the English and Scottish Governments follow suit.

Resources). The only stipulations are that if you have a coffin, it is of a type that does not release harmful toxins when it breaks down, and embalmed bodies are often not accepted for the same reason. The graves are single depth and shallow to allow the most efficient breakdown of the bodies back to the earth.

The same movement exists in the US and you can find out details at the Green Burial Council (see 'Useful contacts' in the Resources).

Home burials/private land

I had no idea that we could have buried DD at home on our own patch of land, which I imagine would cut burial costs considerably! You *don't* have to register the grave on the UK Land Registry and councils *don't* have the right to demand details or charge, nor do you need planning permission for a 'limited number of interments'. 'Limited', according to the excellent advice from the Natural Death Centre, means no more than two burials, and as I don't imagine you intend to bury a host of your loved ones in your garden, it is therefore not necessary to apply for change of use (to a cemetery, I presume)! It is, however, advisable to notify the police before the burial, as neighbours may worry if they see you in the garden reading out the helpful online pdf on 'Digging a Grave' and leaning on a large shovel! There are also considerations if you're close to a public footpath…[3]

If you are seriously considering this, do give some thought to what you will do if you ever had to sell the property, as negotiating the right to visit the grave will obviously cause complications in your sale. If you still want to go ahead:

- You will need to be the freeholder of the property (or have their consent).

- There must be no restrictive covenants attached to the title deeds/registration of the property that prohibit burial.

---

3   The Natural Death Centre's website has details (see Resources).

- Speak to your local council's environmental health department to check that the burial will not take place within certain distances of specific types of water.[4]

- The slip attached to the bottom of the Certificate for Burial must be completed and returned to the Registry within 96 hours of burial.

- The owner of the land (or agent) must keep the burial register in a safe place.

If you're in the US, again check the laws in your state for any permits that might be required.

Direct burial

This is for people who feel they do not need a formal, public, ceremonial burial. The body is buried without any procession, without any kind of service and with no one present. The ceremony could happen elsewhere at a later date. I can't imagine a child or young person would ever be buried with no one present...

CREMATION
Challenging common misconceptions

- Your child does *not* have to be cremated if they have had cancer or their body was embalmed.

- Ashes do *not* get mixed up at the crematorium. Even neonates and babies can have their ashes recovered and returned to parents except in unbelievably rare circumstances. If you are at all worried this might be the case, discuss it with your crematorium director. For miscarried and stillborn babies, fortunately there is now a

---

4   Details can be found under 'Private land burial' on the Natural Death Centre's website (see Resources).

specialised crematorium service available in the UK where you can have a personalised casket (see Resources for contact details). The best advice[5] for very low gestational age babies is to place them in a wooden casket and perhaps add a metal disk with your baby's name, so you can be sure the ashes will be recovered at your local crematorium. The charity Sands does say that hospital funerals at crematoria do sometimes cremate several miscarried babies together and will not be able to give parents ashes back, but parents should be told where the ashes will be buried or scattered.

• You *don't* have to close the curtain during the service at a crematorium (this utterly freaked me out as a young teen when my grandfather died).

• You *don't* have to have a service at the crematorium to honour their life if you want your child's body to be cremated. You can just organise for the body to be transported to the crematorium and collect the ashes afterwards for a separate ceremony of your choosing. This is called direct cremation. (It has the added advantage of cutting costs.) This was what we did for DD.

• An open-air pyre is *not* illegal! In 2010, a Hindu, Mr Davender Ghai, won the right to be cremated in accordance with his religious beliefs at the Court of Appeal in London. In fact, the original Cremation Act of 1902 was in part due to the passionate and theatrical legal defence mounted by a heartbroken Welsh doctor, William Price. His toddler died in 1884 and Price cremated him atop a Welsh mountain and was instantly arrested. He argued there was no legislation against what he had done, was acquitted and, on his own death in 1893, had a triumphant hilltop cremation attended by some 20,000 spectators with a special song and postcard to commemorate the occasion. I have no idea how you

---

5   From the Institute of Cemetary and Crematorium Management (ICCM).

would actually go about this – you'll have to ring the Natural Death Centre for detailed legal advice!

Requirements for cremation

In the UK you will need:

- An application for cremation form signed by the next of kin.

- Two cremation forms for which you are charged a fee:[6]

  1. a medical certificate completed by the doctor treating the child during their last illness/death – they must see the body. This doctor does not have to have signed the MCCD.

  2. a confirmatory medical certificate completed by a second doctor registered for at least five years who cannot be a partner/work colleague of the first.

- A certificate signed by the medical referee at the crematorium to authorise cremation. This professional has the power to refuse and order a post-mortem and/or refer the matter to the coroner or procurator fiscal (Scotland).

- Please note that the equipment at some crematoria can't handle a shroud without a firm board underneath (a charging board). Check with your crematorium. If that is the case, the Respect Everybody Shroud has been designed to cater for this.[7]

If you're in the US, again check the laws in your state for any permits that might be required.

---

6   These charges may be abolished when the new requirements by government come into force.

7   See 'Other useful resources'.

Scattering the ashes or 'cremains'

I know this really belongs under 'Ceremonies' (below) but somehow it felt right to put it here. Looking online, you come across all manner of stories describing how a family scattered the ashes of someone they loved and unusual and creative ways to present them. People have had special pouches made in teddies, put them in jewellery, into shotgun shells, fireworks and even launched them at vast cost into lunar orbit in a rocket. The sky is literally the limit! Most of Callum's ashes are in a 'memory bear', but Jane says some went to family plots in the UK and US.

Please note the following:

- If you wish to take your child's ashes abroad to scatter them, be aware that many countries have strict rules on their importation, so it's important to check before travelling.

- If you wish to scatter your child's ashes on private land, you need the permission of the landowner.

CEREMONIES

This is so personal and covers such a huge range of religious and non-religious practice that I feel I can only describe my experience and present that of other families.

I have been honoured to have been present at a few funerals of children of friends in my lifetime. A few details have really stuck in my memory, through my tears. One young girl was buried in the wedding dress for the ceremony she would never live to see. I loved that a six-year-old's funeral stipulated everyone should wear his favourite colour of red: *no* black. His young friends had all painted fabulous pictures for him that had been clothes-pegged to lines strung down the aisle and very young guests had pictures to colour within the order of service.

Another mother wanted very much to speak but worried she would not be able to manage during the service, so she recorded herself at home in the days before reading out a favourite story. That was so beautiful.

All of the above took place in the local church and involved flowers, readings, music and pictures by the people who loved and knew them. In all three, the body was present in a flower-wreathed coffin of some sort. The young children present all appeared to enjoy themselves enormously; the adults didn't but knew they had to be there. Life is suffering.

For DD, a church ceremony would have been most inappropriate, given his Buddhist beliefs. We had erected an enormous marquee in the neighbour's field and the word went out to the community (via my neighbour) that a lot of cake was going to be required – it was The Great British Bake-off Celebration! A girlfriend who runs a catering company organised ice cream, sandwiches, tea, coffee and wine on tap, and a couple of Portaloos. Four hundred people arrived for a celebration tea. DD's friends had painted prayer flags which hung all around the marquee and are now decaying flamboyantly in the wood below our house that DD loved so much. Taking pride of place, on a table in the centre of a raised dais, with pictures of him screening on a loop as a backdrop, were his ashes in the box Holly had decorated. There was a huge bowl of sand with incense sticks for anyone to light and display in his honour, buckets for donations to CLIC Sargent and the Brain Tumour Charity, and piles of blood and organ donation forms with pens to fill them in.

I remember very little except snapshots: children playing football outside or running around, dripping ice cream in hand followed by a hopeful dog; trying to face walking down a parted crowd with 'Shine on You Crazy Diamond' playing on the sound system, and comforting Holly at one point. The 'service' – if you could call it that – was led by our friend Wai Man, as I realised people would not otherwise know what was expected of them at a Buddhist-Lite ceremony! He first read out Buddha's Words of Loving Kindness and then announced what was coming next. George, a life-long friend of DD's, read out a funny poem DD had written about school; Aunty read out the Ben Jonson poem (see dedication page) and I gave the eulogy (see 'My Eulogy for DD'). I know that sounds crazy, but I needed to. I took the precaution of giving Wai a copy with the sections underlined where I tended to cry, so that he could step in until I had recovered. Every time I had practised reading it aloud, I had broken down, but incredibly, on the day, people laughed and that relaxed me and I was able to continue and finish. I had not realised it was laugh-out-loud funny. The Celebration finished with Wai leading some Buddhist prayers and the Beatles added 'With a Little Help from My Friends'. DD would have loved the whole thing.

His ashes are still, four years later, up in his room but get moved to our room when we have guests. It's not a shrine and it hasn't been left exactly as DD had it. Holly uses it for sleepovers, as it's a bigger room than hers. His ashes are complicated; my feelings have changed and continue to. The fact that we have still not scattered them is something I know some friends worry about, and I'm guessing they think it must mean we haven't 'moved on'. I like to correct that language to 'moved forward', as to me moving on implies leaving someone behind and I like to think DD is still, and will always be, with us moving forward – if you see what I mean. There was a moment, about a year after he died, when I thought I could face scattering his ashes, but Toby couldn't and now I don't think we will. We like having him around. Wai was telling us that some Chinese keep their ashes instead of burying or scattering them; Buddhism makes no particular spiritual distinction about where the ashes are placed. Hungry Ghost Day is a traditional Chinese festival on the fifteenth day of the seventh month to honour all deceased, including the same and younger generations. I *love* that concept! DD loved food so I can see him coming on that day to his set place at the table as a particularly hungry ghost! (DD would write three or four exclamation marks here but I think the editor will stop me!!)

Theresa and Asher

For a long time I didn't have anything from Theresa for this section, so I thought maybe she didn't want to discuss it, but I thought I'd better double-check before I sent off the manuscript…

> Are you kidding?!? We threw *a party*!! No funeral. A Celebration of Life. Attendees were instructed *not* to wear black, only bright colors. Those who knew us really well actually wore super hero t-shirts! It was awesome! Nearly 300 people packed the church. We had six priests conducting the service. To put that into perspective, that many priests saying mass is usually reserved for really important people. Well, I guess Asher was. I created a PowerPoint slide show of him accompanied by his favorite music from Disney movies like *Madagascar* and *Cars*, to Aerosmith, to Johnny Cash, to MC Hammer. We decorated the tables with photos of Asher in bright frames in all shapes and sizes. Those who wanted to take them home were encouraged to. We also had a display table of his favorite toys, books, and stuffed animals – all things Asher. Every year we celebrate his birthday with homemade banana pudding (his favorite) and sing 'Happy Birthday' to him.

Alison and Ryan

Alison, like me, derives enormous comfort from still having Ryan's ashes with her, seven years after his death. They're in a memorial bear which they've named Rybear – a memorial teddy bear with a special pouch.[8] They go to the annual Memorial Day at Hope House and have raised tens of thousands of pounds in Ryan's memory for the hospice in order that other families may receive the care and support they did. Like me, she is passionate that families have the right information and support for end-of-life care and that itself is part of Ryan's legacy.

---

8   See 'Other useful resources', p.178.

Michelle and Keir

Among our family, friends, acquaintances and others who attended Keir's funeral, it's held up as the 'gold standard' of funerals. Not because it was super fancy, ultra-expensive or held in a grand venue. It was because we arranged it ourselves (with the help of a great funeral director) and it summed up Keir's life really well with a mixture of music, personal reflection and spoken words from family and friends.

As you are no doubt aware (I think I've mentioned it several times already), we are not religious at all and neither was Keir, so we didn't want any reference to any kind of god or other supernatural being in his celebration. Keir was at home with us for a week after he died, so the funeral director brought his coffin to us on the morning of his funeral and we placed him gently into it. It was made of wicker, very much like the Moses basket that we used when he was a baby, and seemed slightly less bleak than a traditional wooden casket.

We had asked our close friends and family to put some special things into his coffin that meant something to both them and Keir. So he went on his way with photographs of his cousins, messages and teddy bears from his best friends, a special card from us that we had all written together, a large multipack of his beloved Haribo Starmix – his sweets of choice prior to losing his swallow (in fact, looking back I wonder if he wasn't slightly addicted to them!) and, lastly, a massive wooden stick, rather like the one that Gandalf carries in *Lord of the Rings*. Keir had a penchant for collecting sticks in his younger years and he also loved *The Lord of the Rings*, so it was a win-win (the stick was provided by my dad). When it was time to go to the crematorium, the funeral director placed the wicker lid on the coffin and they carried him to the waiting hearse. That was so hard. He was leaving us for the final time.

We had asked for family flowers only, with donations to go to two special charities that were close to our hearts and had helped us along our journey. The flowers we got were so apt for him. He had his name picked out in white chrysanthemums, a sword (another obsession), the word 'friend' which was a gift from all his primary school friends, various other more traditional displays and finally a huge floral SpongeBob Squarepants. That cartoon could make him laugh like nothing else (except my dad).

The ceremony itself was a little bit of a blur at first. I honestly can't remember walking into the crematorium hall. We had planned who was going to carry Keir in his coffin. Erin and I followed behind. We had also enlisted the help of two of our best friends to kind of emcee the service and keep it running smoothly. We had done an order of service with Keir's photograph on it and these were handed out as people walked in. My brother had borrowed a white screen and projector and we had put together a montage of photographs to show during a moment of quiet reflection.

One of Keir's best friends spoke first and then it was our turn. None of us felt that we would be able to make it through a eulogy, so we all nominated someone close to us to read it on our behalf – though on reflection afterwards Erin joked that if she had done it herself, she would've probably cried less than her friend Lucy who read it for her. When Lucy stepped down after her reading, she had huge track marks down her face where her tears had blazed a trail through her foundation. We all found this highly amusing – as the man himself would no doubt have done. When my dad used to look after Keir on a Tuesday (pre-illness), they would go swimming. Keir loved the pool and was an amazing swimmer. He especially loved to swim underwater. This now makes complete sense as he must have felt weightless and the constraints of his body were no longer an issue (even pre-diagnosis, his mobility and coordination weren't the best). My dad would say, 'Come on, Keir, time to go', and he would reply, 'Just five more minutes, Grandad', and my dad would acquiesce. At the end of his eulogy, my dad simply said, 'Just five more minutes, Keir, but it wasn't to be'. He loved him so much.

Martin had chosen the music over the years – you do this when you know what's coming: you plan. It couldn't have been more perfect. The lyrics of the songs were poignant, sometimes sombre, uplifting, positive and tragic all at once. There were no hymns.

We chose a crematorium that allowed 45 minutes for the service (some only offer 20–30-minute slots which we felt were not long enough for our purposes). When the service was over, our clever funeral director asked everybody to leave first, leaving just us in the room. I have to say, it took rather a long time for everyone to leave as the place was packed, but it was a moment for us to catch our breath before that last goodbye. That was *the* hardest moment – I didn't want to leave and accept that finality. He was leaving all over again.

We had his wake at a local pub which is run by a friend of ours. When we arrived, there was a huge photo of Keir on the bar and the place was filled with SpongeBob balloons. Afterwards, we had a gathering at our house and set off some huge fireworks – another favourite. I feel that we did him proud that day. It was right for him and it was right for us.

I would like to share some of the lyrics to one of the songs we chose for his funeral which sums up the sentiment of the day, of us as a family and of Keir himself:

Do you realize
That you have the most beautiful face?
Do you realize
We're floating in space?
Do you realize
That everyone you know, someday, will die?
And instead of saying all of your goodbyes,
Let them know you realise that life goes fast,
It's hard to make the good things last.
You realise the sun doesn't go down,
It's just an illusion caused by the world spinning round.[9]

---

9   From 'Do You Realize?' by the Flaming Lips.

And boy was he a good thing!

We couldn't save Keir, but he saved us, saved me. Keir Michael Henry Platt, my treasure, my hero, my son.

Jane and Callum

I gave a eulogy at Callum's funeral, which made people laugh and smile – which sums up my Puds completely. We also had a balloon release; two funny stories there – one of Callum's carers brought a giant Minion balloon which was whipped out of his hand prior to the service by a random gust of wind… and blue foil star-shaped balloons were Callum's favourite. At the release, all of them flew away – apart from a blue foil, star-shaped balloon which hovered for a few moments and then followed the rest. So utterly convinced he was there with us.

CONCLUSION

You are not alone and you can do it (remember Sir Ranulph Fiennes in Chapter 1). You only have one chance to get it right, and as Cicely Saunders, founder of the modern hospice movement observed, 'How people die remains in the memory of those who live on.'[1] Make an excellent plan for your child's end of life as soon as possible and then forget about it and just live and follow your child in whatever they want to do.

This is a plea, a prayer to anyone, anywhere, involved in commissioning and designing palliative and end-of-life care services for children and young people. It is outrageous that currently it is luck that dictates whether you manage a good death for your child. The general public are unaware of this and assume children and young people have been taken care of first and their services are properly organised. To ensure these children and young people have the best quality of life possible, we need paediatric palliative care to be organised at a national level and formally funded in the UK and US. This would result in comprehensive and robust networks of services to support the most disadvantaged and vulnerable young people in our countries, not just a few patches of excellence. Without these, choice in end-of-life care is meaningless. Adults overwhelmingly say, when asked, that they want to die at or near home, provided the services are there to support them; what child or young person would choose otherwise?

---

1   Saunders, C. (1984) 'Pain and impending death.' In: Wall, P. and Melzack, R. (eds.) *Textbook of Pain*. London: Churchill Livingstone.

No parent should receive an incurable diagnosis for their child requiring palliative support without a palliative specialist at that meeting: it has to start at the very beginning. This was true for only *one* family in this book; the networks were in place locally so that their choices, both before and after death, could be delivered. We all dream of the day their experience is all our experience. A good death is priceless.

DD's favourite Buddhist-inspired phrase was: Life is suffering but every second of life is a miracle.

THE END

My Eulogy for DD

What is she doing speaking at her son's memorial, I hear you worry? Well (a) I couldn't ask my poor sister, who has already done so much, or close friends – it's too hard, and Toby couldn't – he cried right through our wedding! (b) We've done nearly five years – from 24 October 2007 to be precise – so I've had a long time to think about this. Grief started at the beginning, so to a certain extent we're used to it. (c) We're too tired to explain to someone else what needs to be said. So don't you worry, I'll bump along somehow, and if I lose it, I'll just pass temporarily along to the wonderful Wai Man.

Why the field – the marquee? To answer, I'm going to have to use a word I dislike – appropriate – it always sounds so dull. It is the appropriate place for DD. What would be *in*appropriate for DD would be for this to take place in the village church, lovely though it is. He pleaded to be allowed a sky burial off Fontmell Tower, as this would have taken in two of his passions – Buddhism and birds of prey. 'Oh, come on, Mum! Let me ask the vicar?' said with the irrepressible grin and mischievous gleam in his eye that we all know so well. 'No you jolly well may not!' I remonstrated. 'The kind villagers of Fontmell would be entirely put off their breakfast seeing bits of you borne aloft by crows – a Dorset village is a far cry from vultures off isolated Tibetan mountain tops.'

DD became interested in Buddhism early in his treatment – we don't quite know how or why. He said he followed the teachings of Buddha rather than being a practising Buddhist. My maternal grandmother converted to Buddhism in the 1950s but

DD never knew her. Wai Man and Xinran had something to do with it. Maybe my appalling lapsed Protestantism didn't help or perhaps it did, depending on which way you look at it! All I do know is that DD's Buddhism helped him immensely. He would curl up on his hospital bed and meditate when things were really out of control – when an operation was delayed, for example. 'All human desire leads to suffering, Mum', he would say. Yeah, even the flipping desire for an operation to *please* not be delayed again, I would mutter fractiously under my breath at his bedside. In these very difficult situations, it was abundantly clear to me just how much more grown-up my child was compared to me. If I was going to do more than just survive, *if* I wanted to support my family mentally, physically and emotionally as well as I possibly could, I knew it would somehow flow from listening to my child (and sometimes the other children on the ward) and *not* to my grown-up neuroses and expectations.

Listening to DD meant enabling his passions: the WWF to whom he gave all his pocket money from an early age and, enthusiast that he was, persuaded Holly and Rufus to do the same. When he found out he was going to die in May, he bequeathed all his savings to them and was always thrilled to find this out later when his dementia meant he had forgotten he had made this arrangement. He was immensely concerned with the state of our beautiful planet and endeavoured to leave this world with the smallest carbon footprint possible. He was constantly thinking or reading about how to live and work sustainably and about the conservation of threatened habitats. His love of Biology and Chemistry, which he was going to study at A Level this term at his beloved school, would have been used to work in this area – of that Toby and I have no doubt at all. This field therefore represents his love of nature.

Now this is all lovely, but it is also where I have to admit Toby and I could find it a bit of a challenge. For example, in hospital I would naturally be held accountable for my WHSmith sandwich packaging as DD knew there were no recycling facilities on the ward. He held *me* particularly in high esteem – I'm supposed to be Miss Eco, you see – but, of course, miserable and fed-up, my standards would have slipped and I'd then find myself rummaging around in the bins retrieving my sorry packet of sandwiches, ramming them into my overnight case to be disposed of appropriately at home. Then there was his excitement about Hugh Fearnley-Whittingstall's *Fish Fight*. This was first screened the night DD had been attached to a noisy seventies machine that separated his blood into its component parts so that his stem cells could be collected for the transplant. We'd had a bad day. He was exhausted, I was the same and we'd just been told that the Blood Bank estimated not nearly enough had been collected on that first day to make the entire proceeding viable. I was down and out in my glass of wine and hoping he'd settle for a nice easy movie but oh no. 'When's Hugh on, Mum? You *do* know which channel it's on? Have you got the government petition we have to sign up on your computer?' That was typical. Yes, I'm afraid all of you, if you love him – and I know many of you do, very much – are going to have to put up with him sitting on your shoulder when you supermarket shop, whispering in your ear as you reach for a product: Is that the Fairtrade one? Is that recyclable packaging? Oh come on, the other one's not *that* much more expensive…

Following the recycling theme, one of the things that most upsets Toby and me is that not one single one of DD's organs can be transplanted to save the life of another child. He would have loved that. The 17-year-old niece of one of our dear friends has just been given a new 20-year lease of life from cystic fibrosis following a double lung transplant. Three people die every day before they get the transplant they need and that process of waiting must be hell – and it kills Toby and me that because DD's organs have been so poisoned and because of the cancer spread we cannot help. So, just in case *anyone* here has always *meant* to sign up to the NHS organ donor register or to give blood and hasn't got around to it, I've got loads of forms for both over there and biros. So you can have a cuppa and cake, fill one out and stick it in the box and I'll post them. Even one form would make us *very* happy. If there are loads left at the end, please do grab a handful and pass them around at your next dinner party – you never know! As far as the need for blood goes, the four-year-old following DD with the same cancer had upwards of 50 blood transfusions during his 15-month treatment – we had a few dozen. I think that gives you some idea.

DD's other passions – food, owls, his friends, his guitar, Taekwondo, surfing, Honeybuns our dog, our two cats, his brother and sister and, of course, his beloved bees, with which Holly has sensibly decorated his biodegradable 'urn'. We told him the day before he died that Dave Longfoot had extracted lots of jars of honey that day, and if DD had still been up, a lid would have been off and a teaspoon would have been passed around. Pure DD Joy. That and watching *The Young Ones* or *Father Ted*, *The IT Crowd* or *Family Guy* and reading Terry Pratchett books. And this is the thing, he knew exactly who he was, who he loved and he *loved* his life. He kept saying at the end that although it was a real shame he couldn't stay, he'd had a *great* time and he knew that many children can't say that. You and I know that many *grown-ups* can't say that. DD knew he was lucky and that is why this *has* to be celebration. His only regret was not being able to do A Levels and go to university. He didn't regret having cancer; in fact, after he had read Lance Armstrong's account of surviving, DD announced that he was glad he had cancer because he reckoned it had made him nicer, especially to his brother. Toby and I hope we're as short of regrets on our death beds.

Toby was very upset the evening before DD died because he said we'd failed – as in the treatment failed – and I think that might be something many people might think. But I hope I manage to persuade you that given how little is understood about how and why brain tumours work as they do and that therefore so much is still guesswork, actually we have triumphed. Maybe one day we'll learn that DD's fingered tumour was a multiforme and actually needed an entirely different approach whose medical particulars are far, far in the future. On *that* basis, care of the patient is the important thing and there we really have triumphed. If you consider that DD spent a *quarter* of his life undergoing some sort of treatment or recovering from one, and then finally dying, the proportion of that time spent at home then becomes *critically* important. And the fact is that due to excellent management by the multi-disciplinary team at Southampton General Hospital, linked to Salisbury District Hospital for lesser infections and procedures and then to our GP and the district nurses at Abbeyview Medical Centre, DD managed to spend a fantastic amount of time at home as an outpatient. This has to be the way forward for all cancer patients, not just children, and it shouldn't have anything to do with postcodes. It does involve trust all round – we trusted the medical team and, just as important, they trusted Toby and I, and DD trusted us. For this level of professional care, our medical teams, some of whom I know are here today, have earned Toby's and my undying gratitude. If any of them – our oncologist's wife's brother's niece's half-sister even – needed something, Toby and I would die of gratitude to be able to do something in return.

By 'we' triumphed, I also mean family and all of you – his friends and community – as well as the specialist charities that support families like ours. CLIC Sargent are absolutely on the frontline in helping families try and normalise life during cancer treatment. We lived for weeks at times in their haven – an immaculate hostel in the hospital car park – as our round trip from home was three hours in traffic (seven in snow). It operated as a halfway house if DD was not so ill he had to be admitted but I was a tad anxious and too tired to drive, for example. There was also room for Holly and Rufus, which was particularly helpful on birthdays. Marie Curie don't normally look after children, but I am informed that if there is a good care plan in place and the requisite permissions, they do. Well, I can tell you unequivocally that the ten nights they came in right at the end ensured that DD had a good death, because it meant Toby and I could sleep and then be able to cope looking after him during the day. There is just no substitute for professionals and the two nurses we had were paragons whose sainthoods are clearly well advanced.

At home it was all of you – friends, family and community – that kept our family strong: prayers of all denominations, food, booze, flowers, sweets, cleaning help, looking after the dog, dealing with complex welfare payments, visits, teaching DD at home, teaching DD at school, doing the bees with DD, making pots with DD, staying up all night with DD, making sure I rang C Neuro when shunts were misbehaving, helping me get DD to the prom, laying wreaths for and lighting candles for DD; friends climbed mountains for us, took us on holiday, organised helicopters for us, invited us out, scooped up Holly and Rufus, housed relatives, drove us, rang to check up on us, ran my choirs, massaged and stretched me, sold and edited my books, baked cakes, at all times ran with my obsession with the vital HeadSmart campaign, taught me how to Facebook and Tweet to raise awareness; even Toby's inmates – supposedly the baddest of the bad – have written songs to raise awareness and funds for HeadSmart for him. In short, there has been *nothing* you would not do to help. So don't you dare wonder how I can stand up here and function, because it's entirely your fault!

So as far as we are concerned, our family has been the embodiment of perfectly executed care in the community and we should absolutely celebrate. We're only too well aware how rare this is and how lucky we've been. To have achieved the life DD wanted and the death – he wanted to be at home, helping out, then be cremated and have his ashes sprinkled around the pool in the hazel wood – is really something. He was calm and comfortable right to the end – the unswerving aim of Toby and I and the medical team. I think for DD 'P' didn't stand for palliative care, it stood for party – and he was dining next to the prettiest girl at supper the week he died. Knowing this and that he, we, did *everything* we possibly could gives us a real sense of closure – again something denied many others. The fact, then, that DD, as he so inimitably put it in that TV interview, was then 'kind of stuffed but hey, you can't win them all!' is terribly sad but it's also kind of irrelevant. I know we will never stop missing him but then, as a friend put it, that's not a death sentence; it's a life sentence – to remember all the good things. And my goodness there are *so many* good things and you will all have your own memories of him. I found this and it really made me laugh: DD had been asked to write about electricity in year two, aged six; this is the first paragraph![1] He's already won a faster diagnosis for the next generation of children unfortunate enough to have brain tumours by his willingness to speak out when he was dying. And, mysteriously, Dave the beekeeper says there's now a new queen with a new colony in what was an empty hive – DD knew there would be.

I'll end with perhaps his favourite Buddhist phrase: Life is suffering but every second of life *is* a miracle. If you could learn to live in the moment, as he did, he would be so very happy for you – it made him happy despite everything he went through. DD *lived strong*, in the words of Lance Armstrong's cancer foundation, but just as important he *died strong*.

Thank you all.

---

1   Airlectrisety
    Electricity can be very dangerus.
    Babyies sometimes put there fingers in socets and get electricyooted and then die.
    But, it can be yousful.
    (His teacher gave him a star!)

Resources

SOME ABBREVIATIONS AND TERMS

AAHPM American Academy of Hospice and Palliative Medicine. This is the professional organisation for professionals specialising in hospice and palliative medicine.

AAP American Academy of Pediatrics. The professional association of pediatricians.

ACP Advance Care Plan (see Chapter 2) – a voluntary document (legally binding in the US).

AD Advance Decision/healthcare directive (also known as a living will, medical directive, personal directive) – a legally binding document. It can be revoked and changed at any time.

ADR (UK) Alternative Dispute Resolution and Mediation Services.

CAFCASS (UK) Children and Family Court Advisory and Support Service

CANH Clinically Assisted Nutrition and Hydration. May be provided by naso-gastric or naso-jejunal tube (also known as an NJ tube) – a fine tube inserted into your small bowel via your nose. The tube can then be used to deliver liquid feed, water and medications into your small bowel.

CCC (US) Complex Chronic Conditions.

CCLG (UK) Children's Cancer and Leukaemia Group.

CCN (UK) Community Children's Nurse.

CDOP (UK) Child Death Overview Panel.

CEC (UK) Clinical Ethics Committee.

CPIR (US) Center for Parent Information and Resources (formerly NICHCY – National Dissemination Center for Children with Disabilities).

CPN (UK) Community Practice Nurse – senior staff nurses who do further management training to become community nurses.

CPAP Continuous Positive Airway Pressure – a means of respiratory ventilation used for the critically ill with breathing difficulties. It can prevent the need for tracheal intubation.

CPR Cardiopulmonary Resuscitation – violent chest compressions and electric paddles applied to shock the heart into starting after it has stopped.

DNR/DNAR Do Not Resuscitate/Do Not Attempt Resuscitation.

DNACPR Do Not Attempt CPR – applies only to attempts to restart the heart and lungs in the event of cardiorespiratory arrest.

DN (UK) District Nurse – has university degree-level specialism in district nursing.

EOLC End-of-Life Care.

Gillick Test (UK law) The Gillick test is commonly used to ascertain whether a child (aged 16 years or younger) is able to consent to his or her own medical treatment, with or without the need for parental consent and/or knowledge. For the child to be Gillick competent, the child must have sufficient maturity and understanding to take a decision of the seriousness in question.[1]

GP (UK) General Practitioner. This is our first call – primary care – in the UK when we are sick. They refer us on to specialist NHS doctors at the hospitals.

HC (US) Hospice Care.

HCP (UK) Health Care Professional.

HDU High-Dependency Unit – where patients need single organ support (excluding mechanical ventilation). In the UK they are staffed on a ratio of one nurse to two patients. Sometimes beds are combined within the ICU.

HTA (UK) Human Tissue Authority.

ICU Intensive Care Unit – where patients require support for two or more organs or need mechanical ventilation alone. In the UK, they are staffed with one nurse per patient and usually with a doctor present in the unit 24 hours per day.

ITU Intensive Therapy Unit (also known as ICU).

LLC (US) Life-Limiting Condition – a childhood condition where the child is not expected to live to adulthood.[2]

LTC (US) Life-Threatening Condition – a very serious threat to the wellbeing of the child; prognosis questionable (see LLC above).

LSCB (UK) Local Safeguarding Children's Boards.

LST Life-Sustaining Treatment. This previously stood for life-saving treatment, but was amended by the RCPCH to show that the treatment is not curative but palliative/supportive.

MCA (England and Wales) Mental Capacity Act 2005. In Scotland, the Adults with Incapacity Act 2000 provides the statutory framework and in Northern Ireland decision making is still governed by common law.

MCCD (UK) Medical Certification of Cause of Death.

MD (US) Doctor of Medicine.

MDT (UK) Multidisciplinary Team. All the specialist health care professionals looking after you/your child.

MOLST (US) Medical Order for Life-Sustaining Treatment (see POLST below).

NIH (US) National Institutes of Health.

NHFA (US) National Home Funeral Alliance.

NHPCO (US) National Hospice and Palliative Care Organization.

NICE (UK) National Institute for Health and Care Excellence.

NICU Neonatal Intensive Care Unit.

NNU Neonatal Unit.

NP (US) Nurse Practitioner.

NPAF (US) National Patient Advocate Foundation. Free, not-for-profit service offering advice on all aspects of the US healthcare system.

---

1   See Archives of Disease in Childhood, 'Making decisions to limit treatment in life-limiting and life-threatening conditions in children: A framework for practice', http://adc.bmj.com/content/100/Suppl_2/s1.

2   Sarah Freibert, MD, and Conrad Williams, MD, 'NHCPO's Facts and Figures: Pediatric Palliative and Hospice Care in America', 2015 edition, published by the National Hopsice and Palliative Care Association, www.nhpco.org/sites/default/files/public/quality/Pediatric_Facts-Figures.pdf.

NPCRC (US) National Palliative Care Research Center. This is committed to stimulating, developing and funding research directed at improving care for seriously ill patients and their families.

ODR (UK) Organ Donor Register.

OT Occupational Therapy/Therapist.

PA (US) Physician's Assistant.

PALS (UK) Patient Advice and Liaison Service.

PASS Patient Advice and Support Service – the Scottish equivalent of PALS.

PFC (US) Partners for Children – California's public pediatric community-based palliative care benefit.

PICU Paediatric Intensive Care Unit.

PHE (UK) Public Health England.

PM Post-Mortem.

PoD Place of Death.

POLST (US) Physician's Orders for Life-Sustaining Treatment. This form is voluntary and has no age limit. A child can have one. It is signed by the patient/parent and clinician, and it clearly states what kinds of medical treatment the patient wants/wants to refuse at the end of life. It includes DNR decisions.

PP (US) Pediatric Palliative.

RCPCH (UK) Royal College of Paediatrics and Child Health.

ReSPECT (UK) **Re**commended **S**ummary **P**lan for **E**mergency **C**are and **T**reatment. This is a personalised recommendation for clinical care in emergency situations where the patient is not able to make decisions or express their wishes. It goes alongside the more detailed ACP. It's new in the UK and is being trialled in 2017 in a few areas.

RN (US) Registered Nurse.

SOI (UK) Statement of Intent. Form signed by the GP who must be sure that death is both expected and imminent, and that the death will be from natural causes. It has to be reviewed every fortnight.

USEFUL CONTACTS
UK

A Child of Mine – www.achildofmine.org.uk
> Set up by bereaved parents after their child died of cancer, this charity supports parents suffering the loss of their baby and child. Practical information, guidance and support are all there: help for siblings and grandparents and inspiration for funerals – transport, songs, eulogies, orders of service and floral tributes.

Ask the Expert – https://community.macmillan.org.uk/cancer_experiences/ask_the_expert
> Ask the Expert is Macmillan's online community support. You can ask a huge range of experts – nurse specialists, dieticians, consultants and so on – a question and they will endeavour to get back to you within two working days.

Bliss – www.bliss.org.uk
> Charity supporting babies born premature or sick.

Brain UK – www.southampton.ac.uk/brainuk/index.page
> The world's first virtual brain bank. It is essentially a matching service that catalogues in a centralised database brain tissue collected and stored by the network of NHS neuropathology departments across the UK and makes them available for researchers. They catalogue both living tissue and tissue collected post-mortem.

Child Bereavement UK – www.childbereavementuk.org
Child Bereavement UK supports families and educates professionals when a baby or child of any age dies or is dying, or when a child is facing bereavement.

Child Death Helpline – www.childdeathhelpline.org.uk
A Freephone service – 0800 282 986 or 0808 800 6019 – for all those affected by the death of a child.

Child Funeral Charity – www.childfuneralcharity.org.uk
Helps with child funeral costs in the UK. Health professionals can refer families. Depending on financial status, the government also has a social fund available (www.gov.uk/funeral-payments/how-to-claim).

Childhood Bereavement Network – www.childhoodbereavementnetwork.org.uk
The CBN supports professionals working with bereaved children and young people.

CLIC Sargent – www.clicsargent.org.uk
Supporting children with cancer and their families.

Children Are Butterflies – www.childrenarebutterflies.org.uk
This charity provides support – both emotional and financial – to families who have lost children of any age. They have a network of parents in similar situations who can offer support so that 'You Are Not Alone'. They can help with funeral expenses.

Children's Hospices Across Scotland – www.chas.org.uk
CHAS is the charity that provides the only hospice services in Scotland for children and young people. It enables them to enjoy the time they have and helps their families celebrate them and their lives.

Funeralzone – www.funeralzone.co.uk/NHS
Funeralzone is a free online resource for the bereaved.

Lullaby Trust – www.lullabytrust.org.uk
Originally the Foundation for Sudden Infant Death (FSID) – the cot death charity. This charity works with the Department of Health and other healthcare professionals to reduce the number of infant deaths through awareness, professional training and research. It also provides support to bereaved families.

Macmillan Cancer Support – www.macmillan.org.uk
Macmillan is one of the largest British charities. It provides practical, medical and financial support and pushes for better cancer care.

Marie Curie – www.mariecurie.org.uk
The national charity providing care and support for people living with terminal illness and their families. Freephone 0800 090 2309.

National Association of Funeral Directors – www.nafd.org.uk

SANDS Stillbirth and Neonatal Death Charity – www.sands.org.uk
SANDS is a charity supporting anyone affected by the death of a baby, working to improve the care bereaved parents receive, and promoting research to reduce the loss of babies' lives.

Teenage Cancer Trust – www.teenagecancertrust.org
Supporting teenagers and young people with cancer.

The Brain Tumour Charity – www.thebraintumourcharity.org
The largest brain tumour charity in the UK, providing support and information and funding research.

The Digital Legacy Centre – www.digitallegacyassociation.org
Provides guidance for healthcare professionals, patients and their carers on managing social media and other digital assets at the end of life.

The Natural Death Centre – www.naturaldeath.org.uk
Founded in 1991, this charity aims to inform, inspire and empower the public in all matters related to death and dying with a particular focus on raising awareness of choices outside of the mainstream.

Together for Short Lives – www.togetherforshortlives.org.uk
The leading UK charity for all children with life-threatening and life-limiting conditions and all those who support, love and care for them – families, professionals and services.

US

American Academy of Hospice and Palliative Medicine – www.aahpm.org
The organisation that can help parents with children with life-threatening illnesses.

American Association for Marriage and Family Therapy – www.aamft.org.
They have state and provincial divisions where you can look for support.

Center for Parent Information and Resources – www.parentcenterhub.org
Supporting the Parent Centers who serve families of children with disabilities c/o the statewide parent advocacy network (SPAN). It is a hub of information with a website produced by the US Department of Education.

Courageous Parents Network – https://courageousparentsnetwork.org
CPN is an incredible hub of information and support created by families for families caring for children with serious illnesses in the US, though the themes are universal to any parent anywhere. You can watch videos of parents sharing their experiences caring for their seriously ill children, including end of life and bereavement, and talk with other parents online or privately. It also includes professional guidance in the form of short videos, podcasts and blogs by a huge range of health professionals, and you can search by topic or disease.

End of Life Practitioners Collective – www.endoflifepro.org
ELPC describes itself as an 'eclectic mix of practitioners who serve others at end of life' and try to bridge the gap in health and death care. They are described as doulas, midwives, end-of-life guides and coaches. Their Facebook page (www.facebook.com/endoflifepro) is to show the public what they do and where people seeking someone in a particular city can post.

Funeral Consumers Alliance – www.funerals.org
The FCA is a non-profit organization whose goal is 'to ensure consumers are fully prepared and protected when planning a funeral for themselves or their loved ones'.

Green Burial Council – www.greenburialcouncil.org
Green funerals and natural burials.

National Funeral Directors Association – www.nfda.org

National Home Funeral Alliance – www.homefuneralalliance.org
The NHFA is a national, non-profit, volunteer organisation that helps teach families to care for their own after death. It gives legal requirements in your state. It's committed to 'reconnecting to our heritage, educating and empowering families to care for their own at death'.

National Hospice and Palliative Care Organization – www.nhpco.org
NHPCO is the largest non-profit membership organization representing hospice and palliative care programs and professionals. It also advocates for the terminally ill and their families.

National Patient Advocate Foundation – www.npaf.org
> NPAF is dedicated to advancing person-centered care for everyone facing a serious illness. 'We advocate for accessible, high quality, affordable health care.'

Partnership for Parents – www.partnershipforparents.net
> This website is presented by the Coalition for Compassionate Care of California. It describes itself as 'a safety net for parents of children with serious illnesses'.

Patient Advocate Foundation – www.patientadvocate.org www.npaf.org
> PAF is a free, not-for-profit service with the primary purpose of providing mediation and arbitration services to patients, providers, family members and caregivers of those dealing with significant medical issues and the impact on their lives.

The Center for Children with Special Needs – www.cshcn.org
> Started in 1998 as a program of Seattle Children's Hospital, the Center for Children with Special Needs provides information and resources for families and professionals. It primarily serves families in the Pacific North-West.

WISH CHARITIES – UK

I'm just giving websites so you can see exactly what they offer yourself.

Dreams Come True – www.dreamscometrue.uk.com

Family Fund – www.familyfund.org.uk

Family Holiday Association – www.fhaonline.org.uk

Fulfil the Wish – www.fulfilthewish.org

Promise Dreams – www.promisedreams.co.uk (for 0–18 years old)

React – https://reactcharity.org

Roald Dahl's Marvellous Children's Charity – www.roalddahl.com/charity

Round Table Children's Wish – www.rtcw.org

Starlight – www.starlight.org.uk

The Muscle Help Foundation – www.musclehelp.com (for muscular dystrophy)

When You Wish upon a Star – www.whenyouwishuponastar.org.uk (for 2–16 years old)

Willow – www.willowfoundation.org.uk (for 16–40 years old)

WISH CHARITIES – US

Give Kids the World Village – www.givekidstheworld.org
> Give Kids the World Village is an 84-acre, non-profit 'storybook' resort in Central Florida. Here, children with life-threatening illnesses and their families are treated to week-long, cost-free vacations.

Make-a-Wish – www.worldwish.org
> Make-a-Wish America grants wishes for children in the US through its 62 chapters, but since its inception in 1980, it now serves children in nearly 50 countries on five continents.

OTHER USEFUL RESOURCES

Cold cot refrigeration for after death – www.bond-group.com
No hire service available.

Flexmort CuddleCot and CoverCool Mini – http://flexmort.com
Electrical cooling process, not refrigeration. No hire service available.

Love Keep Create – www.lovekeepcreate.co.uk
Makes precious keepsakes from their clothes.

Memorial jewellery

- www.smallprint.com
- www.lastingtouch.co.uk
- www.handonheartjewellery.co.uk
- www.brentjess.com
- www.ashesintoglass.co.uk

Respect Everybody Shrouds – www.respectgb.co.uk

Simpson's Memory Box Appeal (SiMBA) – www.simbacharity.org.uk
Memory boxes for full-term and pre-term babies.

Something Precious: The Smallest Ever Baby Burial Clothes – www.baby-burial-gowns.co.uk

Special Care Foetal Cremations – www.specialcarecremations.co.uk
Memorial services, personalised infant cremation caskets and demise pouches for babies under 24 weeks.

Teddy bear urns/memorials

- www.cami-bear.com
- www.achildofmine.org.uk
- www.inthelighturns.com
- www.ashesandurns.co.uk/shop/cremation-keepsakes/memory-bear-with-ribbon

The Haydon Kennan Foundation – www.haydon.kennon.co.uk
Supplies the hand imprint kits for the SiMBA memory boxes.

Tiny Souls Bereavement Photography – www.tinysouls.org

A FEW PUBLICATIONS

NICE (2016) End of life care for infants, children and young people with life-limiting conditions: planning and management, NICE guideline. www.nice.org.uk/guidance/ng61/resources/end-of-life-care-for-infants-children-and-young-people-with-lifelimiting-conditions-planning-and-management-1837568722885.

NICE (2017) End of life care for infants, children and young people, Quality standard [QS160]. www.nice.org.uk/guidance/qs160/history.

Vic Larcher, Finella Craig, Kiran Bhogal, Dominic Wilkinson, Joe Brierley on behalf of the Royal College of Paediatrics and Child Health (RCPCH) (2015) 'Making decisions to limit treatment in life-limiting and life-threatening conditions in children: A

framework for practice.' *Archives of Disease in Childhood 100*, s1–s23. http://adc.bmj.
com/content/100/Suppl_2/s1.

> This is the framework within which decisions are made in the best interests of the child. It is consistent with UK law. It is intended for health professionals but also to increase understanding in parents and families. It covers all the ethical considerations – parental responsibilities in decision making and the children's rights.

Together for Short Lives (2012) *A Guide to End of Life Care: Care of Children and Young People before Death, at the Time of Death and after Death* (itself an adaptation from *Care of the Child after Death*, Children's Hospices, 2011).

> This is for the professionals but has been invaluable for me to see what they have to do and what it's called!

> If you want to know what children's hospice services are available, Together for Short Lives has a little booklet with all the essential information that's part of a series on many aspects of palliative care for parents and health professionals (www. togetherforshortlives.org.uk). Their guides cover everything from enabling good transition from children's to adult services to neonatal care pathway for babies with palliative care needs. If you can't find what you need on their website, just ring and ask.

Children's Cancer and Leukaemia Group (CCLG) (2015) *Facing the Death of Your Child: Suggestions and Help for Families, Before and Afterwards*. www.cclg.org.uk/write/ MediaUploads/Publications/PDFs/Facing_the_death_of_your_child_(Apr_15).pdf

Children's Cancer and Leukaemia Group (CCLG) (2016) 'Managing Symptoms at Home: Palliative Care Information for Families.' www.cclg.org.uk/publications/search/ managing/Managing-symptoms-at-home/PALLCARE

Linda Goldman (2009) *Great Answers to Difficult Questions about Death: What Children Need to Know* (Jessica Kingsley Publishers).

My favourite book for explaining the idea of death to a very young child: *Duck, Death and the Tulip* by Wolf Erlbrich, Penelope Todd and Catherine Chidgey (Gecko Press, 2007).

My favourite book for discussing palliative care and death but in grown-ups: *Being Mortal: Illness, Medicine and What Matters in the End* by Atul Gawande (Henry Holt and Company, 2014).

Fabulous book on the lives led by children and young people with life-shortening conditions: *Lives Worth Living: Fifteen Stories of Exceptional Children Whose Short Lives Left a Lasting Legacy*, written by their families, with Janet Cotter (Southgate Publishers, 2014).

Integrated Person-Centred Planning for Children, Young People and Families Receiving Palliative Care

GUIDANCE AND TOOLKIT

Rebecca Riley, Rachel Tyler and Sherelle S. Ramus

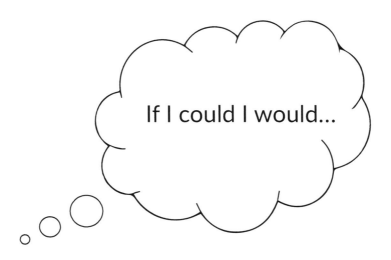

CONTENTS

FOREWORDS

I commend this 'toolkit' to you; it is child-focussed and very family-friendly. Whilst it provides a comprehensive framework, it is not daunting and the information gathered can easily be updated as needed. It is current and very relevant and the format provides an approach to support coordination between services, reviews and transition planning for children, young people and families. It provides a very positive way to tackle some of the challenges and difficult conversations within children's palliative care in a structured, positive and accessible way.

Clare Periton
Chief Executive, Helen & Douglas House Hospice

This practically focussed toolkit for integrated, person-centred planning for children, young people and their families is well aligned with the recent NICE Guidance on End of Life Care for Infants, children and young people with life limiting conditions: Planning and management (NG 61). It provides a practical example of how the guidance on 'Information Sharing', 'Communication', and 'Advance Care Planning' can be put in to everyday practice. In the related Quality Standards (QS 160), NICE have chosen to further highlight the importance of care planning and the active involvement of patients and their families in the process, making this document a helpful vehicle for quality improvement.

Dr Emily Harrop MBBS BSc DCH MRCPCH PhD Dip Pal Med
Consultant in Paediatric Palliative Care
Deputy Chair of the NICE Guideline Development Committee

INTRODUCTION

Support planning for children receiving palliative care, for those living with a life-threatening or limiting illness and their families, using practical person-centred thinking approaches

Person-centred planning (PCP) goes back a long way and has strong links to work promoting independent living (Wolfsenberger 1972). It is based on a social model of illness or disability using a positive, strengths-based approach to support care planning. PCP is defined by O'Brien and Lovett (1992, p.5) as approaches for 'organizing and guiding community change in alliance with people with disabilities and their families and friends... The person at the focus of planning, and those who love the person, are the primary authorities on the person's life direction'. Instead of giving a definition, the Health Foundation (2014) describes 'four principles of person-centred care' which are:

1. Affording people dignity, compassion and respect

2. Offering coordinated care, support or treatment

3. Offering personalised care, support or treatment

4. Supporting people to recognise and develop their own strengths and abilities to enable them to live an independent and fulfilling life.

PCP developed because people with disabilities or long-term conditions often found it difficult to access services, opportunities and experiences and when doing so had to 'fit' into whatever was provided, whether appropriate or not. This approach now has a broader role in integrated care planning, delivery and support across all age groups in many settings. It is important to acknowledge that the PCP approaches and tools exampled in this guidance are well established, They have been developed, researched, tested, refined and recommended over a number of years by many credible sources including the Department of Health (DH) (2010a) and Helen Sanderson and Jaimee Lewis (2011), and are used in health and social care services.

This toolkit aims to help children and families receiving palliative care, and services supporting them, to use person-centred practice. Together for Short Lives (2017, p.1) describe palliative care for children and young people as:

an active and total approach to care, from the point of diagnosis or recognition, embracing physical, emotional, social and spiritual elements through to death and beyond. It focuses on enhancement of quality of life for the child/young person and support for the family and includes the management of distressing symptoms, provision of short breaks and care through death and bereavement.

The Department of Health (2008, p.14) recognises that palliative care for children 'starts at diagnosis and is about improving life experiences for children and young people with life-limiting and life-threatening conditions'. The examples included in this guide are useful for those receiving or 'living with' palliative care support and their support service, to ensure that quality of life is always considered for the child and family along with their health and safety needs. By adopting a more person-centred approach to communication and in planning care, the hope is that this approach will help in other situations when families are involved in planning ahead, such as preparing their child for transition to adult life.

Person-centred planning seeks to create a picture of an individual's life within their family/local community and their choices/hopes, and describe the actions needed to keep moving them in their chosen direction. It provides an approach to care that leads to positive changes in people's lives and services (Ritchie *et al.* 2003). It is about understanding the individual/child/family's values and needs, and how they may be met, rather than thinking about how they will fit into the existing service system. It reaches far beyond service responsibilities to encourage empowerment by considering the actions and responsibilities of the individual child/young person, family and their own personal support network. This is essential for children and families receiving palliative or end-of-life (EoL) care.

Person-centred planning uses a flexible, responsive approach to meeting an individual or family's needs and responds to changing circumstances, guided by the principles of good practice rather than a standard procedure (Sanderson 2000). Person-centred planning is simple and effective. This can help services identify and record unique, useful and important information about an individual and their family, which can prove especially helpful when reviewing ongoing management and palliative support or when having conversations about advance care planning (ACP) or EoL care by:

- providing a clear and practical *focus for discussion* between families and support services

- assisting with identification of *outcomes*

- promoting the use of active listening
- recording information in the child or family's words
- encouraging positive thinking and highlighting individual strengths
- enabling staff and families to find different ways of working, generating creative ideas
- empowering children, young people and their families to be involved, take some control or understand their responsibilities
- helping families to make the right connections
- supporting challenging conversations such as ACP discussions and parallel planning for emergency or end-of-life care.

The word 'child' is used throughout this guidance to refer to babies, children and young people. The word 'support' is used in this guidance to refer to any services, organisation or individuals who provide help for a child/family formally – for example, education, health, social care, charity – or informally, such as family, friends, clubs, etc.

This guidance and toolkit can be used to help put recommendations from the recent NICE Guidance on End of Life Care for Infants, children and young people with life limiting conditions: Planning and management (NG 61) into practice – particularly with regards to information sharing, communication, advance care planning (ACP) and encouraging user and family involvement. This guidance can be used in conversations or to support care planning to help those delivering or receiving longer-term palliative care, emergency or parallel planning. It supports those thinking through ACP, when considering future wishes or choices about where a child may be cared for and who may be involved in giving that care. It can support EoL care planning and delivery. It introduces a number of well-known and well-used person-centred approaches which enable services, families and support networks to think together, have meaningful conversations, gather useful and unique information and help develop care and support plans which aim to achieve a child/young person's and family's desired outcomes/goals and to ensure they live well.

CORE PERSON-CENTRED TOOLS

The first section of this guidance covers a few core person-centred tools that can be used to support children and families receiving palliative care such as:

- *Like and admire* – this conversation can be used to promote positive thinking about a child.

- *Important to and important for* is the principle of how to identify what is important *to* a child/family to achieve happiness/wellbeing and describe good support *for* them to keep healthy and safe.

- *Relationship circles* are used to map and record important relationships – contact information for those people, organisations or services giving a child/family formal and informal support.

- *Working and not working* helps to review a child/family's support and identify any areas for improvement or change. This can help identify outcomes and support reviews of care.

- *One-page profiles* provide a summary of important information about a child. This is useful in any setting to summarise essential care required by the child/family.

1. LIKE AND ADMIRE

Describing what you 'like and admire' about a child is a simple person-centred conversation. This can be used at the beginning of review meetings and gives an opportunity for anyone who knows or supports a child/family to describe in their own words what they like and admire about them. This promotes positive thinking about a child, describing their personality, skills and abilities, and can be included in 'one-page profiles' or other care and support plan documents.

Example: What people said they liked and admired about Hannah at one of her person-centred review meetings at school.

What I like and admire about Hannah is:

- Her relationship with her mum, dad, sister and family.
- She has lots of personality with a smile to melt your heart.
- Hannah is very welcoming and a delight to be around.
- School wouldn't be school without Hannah.
- She enriches everyone's lives.
- Hannah has a strong personality (and will be a strong woman!).
- She is very affectionate with a wicked sense of humour.

2. IMPORTANT TO/IMPORTANT FOR

This tool encourages a way of helping everyone to think about what is *important to* a child or family to promote their wellbeing and ensure they are happy, peaceful and fulfilled (spiritual, emotional and psychological support) and what support is *important for* them to ensure good support to maintain their health and safety. It is important that these elements are balanced if holistic care is to be delivered. If considered in detail, the information recorded can be used to build a 'care plan' which describes all the care and support required by a child. A medication chart would also be needed to support the plan if medications are required.

Important to you for your wellbeing (what you enjoy and what makes you feel happy, peaceful and valued)	Important for you for your health and safety (what good support looks like for you)

Example: A small section of Hannah's important to/for care plan written for use at home to support overnight carers. 'Focusing on things important to and for Hannah helps make things work better for her and for our family' (Rachel Tyler).

What is important to me – what makes me feel happy and valued	Important for me – what good support looks like to keep me safe and healthy
Familiar routines are important as I like to know what is going to happen. **Morning routine:** If I **wake up in the early hours** of the morning, please remove my oxygen and take the probe off my foot but don't turn on the light or open the curtains. Give me a few soft toys to play with, but leave me in my bed and shut the door. If I **wake up later**, it takes me a while to wake up properly. I like to be left in my bed. Once I am ready to get up, please change my nappy and take me to the kitchen for breakfast. **Getting dressed:** I get dressed after my breakfast. I will generally let you get me dressed, as long as you don't rush me. **Lunchtime:** I eat lunch about 12–12.30pm. **After school:** When I get home from school, I am usually happy just sitting on the sofa. I often don't want any toys to play with. **Tea time:** I have tea around 4.30–5pm. **Getting undressed:** Please ask me to put my arms up so that you can undress me. You can also gently encourage me to put my arms up by tapping my elbows. Please do not pull my arms up. **Bath time:** Before my bath I sit on the toilet. I like having a bath, but I hate having my hair washed. Please help me to wash myself. Look out for flying sponges! When it is time to come out of the bath, please dry me. Rub E45 cream on my arms, legs, face and back.	**Support for my breathing** **Overnight oxygen:** I have overnight oxygen every night when I am asleep. I do not like a face mask on my face, so the mask is placed close to my face but not touching it. The oxygen is delivered via a concentrator (supplied from Air Liquide). • I have a high-flow concentrator through which I have 6 litres of oxygen if I have a cold or breathing is difficult. • I have a low-flow concentrator when I am well. I have up to 3 litres. **Saturation monitor:** I have a saturation monitor. • The limits are set for my heart rate at 125 and 46. The limits for the oxygen are set at 100 and 93. • The volume on the monitor is set on level 1 as the alarm is very loud and disturbs my sleep. **Once I have fallen asleep at night, please wait about 20–30 minutes and then put on my oxygen mask and my O2 saturation monitor probe on my toe.** I am normally settled in my sleep for a few hours. However, I do wake very easily so you need to be VERY quiet. **CPAP – Nippy Junior** **Night:** I should use my Nippy every night, but I don't like it. I will keep it on for short periods only when I am awake.

Bedtime: Usually around 7pm, but if tired I will go earlier. I have a drink of milk and a story before I go to bed, with my hip brace on. Sometimes I decide I want to play. I can be active for hours. It is best if you leave me in bed to play. I may shout, but I am quite happy. I sleep with my **little moon light** on all night. I have my **sensory lights** on when I go to bed but please turn them off when I am asleep. If I keep shouting, I may have been to the toilet and need my sleeper pants changing. Sometimes I just want to be reassured that you are there. If I have been shouting for a while, please try to settle me and give me a cuddle. If I fall asleep right at the bottom of the bed, please lift me to the top of the bed and lay me on my front when I am asleep. You will know when I am asleep because you will be able to move me easily without me waking up. **Please put on my oxygen and saturation monitor.**

Daytime: I use my Nippy if I am awake and I have a **'floppy episode'**. If I become very pale, lose my colour, become floppy and unresponsive and my breathing seems shallow, please use my CPAP. It helps to keep my lungs open and you can deliver oxygen through it as well. If I do not come round after 20 minutes, you might want to ring for an ambulance.

Salbutimol Inhaler: I have 2 puffs of my inhaler through a spacer, to help me with my breathing if I can't stop coughing or want to cough but I am not able to do so effectively.

3. RELATIONSHIP CIRCLES

The relationship circle provides a way to visually map out all the important people in a child/family's life. It can be used as a contact sheet and names of people or services can be added along with contact details. Start by drawing some circles on a blank page. Put the child's name in the middle circle. The second circle can be used to identify people who are the closest to the child/family and offer ongoing support. This is close family, parents/carers, siblings, grandparents and close friends whom the family trust and respect and may rely on for support. These people are significant as they will often offer emotional, psychological and/or spiritual support to an individual or the whole family.

The third circle records the names of other people who are very important to the child/family such as more distant relatives – aunts and uncles, cousins, friends, etc. These are individuals who once again are trusted and may be involved in supporting the child/family. Some service providers who give additional levels of one-to-one support or spend significant amounts of time with a child, such as teaching assistants and home carers, may be named in this circle. These may be able to offer objective support or take notes at meetings or when bad news is broken. A further circle can be added for more distant relatives, friends and services if required.

Example: Hannah's relationship circle. 'Information about Hannah is presented in a way that is easy to follow. The details of all contacts are in one place which helps our family and other services to see at a glance who is involved in her care' (Rachel Tyler).

EDUCATION

Blanby School 0113 252525

Alex Hand (Educational Psychologist) 01623 433077

Ash Tree School/Hydrotherapy 0113 252525

Karen Sun (Speech and Language Therapist) Stand Health Centre 0113 252525

Visual Impairment Team Sally Nettle 0113 252525

Occupational Therapy 0113 252525

Inclusion Support Service 0113 467467

PDS 0113 252525

VOLUNTARY

Down's Syndrome Association

Down's Syndrome Speech Group and school for parents

New Life (car seat)

Star Children's Hospice 0133 252525

Janet South, Teaching Assistant, Blanby School 0113 252525

SOCIAL CARE

Karen Bean, Keyworker, Children's Disability Services, Mill House 0113 232323

Denise White, Occupational Therapist, Mill House 0113 343434

Contract Care, short break out of home, Direct payments 0113 474747

OTHERS

Motability – car 0113 467467

Motability Services – outdoor chair/buggy 0114 353535

Hoist Company 0113 454545

Home Adaptations 0550 467467

Home Oxygen Company – Air Liquide 0708 555666

HEALTH CDC

Mrs Taddy, Ophthalmology, CDC 0113 838383 ext 5431

Mr Mend, Community Paediatrician, CDC 0113 838383 ext 5432

Orthotics/Physiotherapy, CDC ext 5436

Sensory Services, CDC 0113 838383

Jo Friend, Physiotherapist, CDC 0113 838383 ext 5437

Children and Adolescent Mental Health Services (CAMHS) 0114 454545

HANNAH'S RELATIONSHIP CIRCLE

(Relationship circle diagram, inner to outer)

Hannah 12 years

Barney (Dog) · Granny Beth · Lily (twin sister) · Ruth (Mum) · Grandad Will · Paul (Dad)

Sharon and family – school friends · John and Rachel – uncle and aunt · Kirsty – friend at school · Nana and Grandpa – Dad's parents (live in Norfolk) · Karen, Simon, Anne and Paul – village friends · Clair – Godmother · Alice, Rick, George and Maisie – family friends

ACUTE HEALTH

Mr Mars, ENG/Audiology, Rope Road 0113 252

Mr Brown, Cardiology 0113 262626

Mr East, Orthopaedics, Great Ormond Street 0113 252525

Mr Fennel, Neurology Children's Hospital 0113 252525

Dr Tell, Respiratory Services, 0113 252525 ext 6256

COMMUNITY HEALTH

GP: Dr Smith 0114 676767

Chiropodist: Mr Jones 0785 676767

Dentist: Halfords 0113 282828

Children's Community Nurses (CCNs) 0113 434343

Home Care – short breaks at home and overnight (Continuing Care): Ruth 0113 95891 ext 62738

The area outside the circles can be used to record people, services and organisations involved with a child/family. These may be services that support the family from social care, education, health voluntary sector and also equipment support services, leisure clubs and social groups, etc. It is helpful to add in titles or roles and contact details such as address, telephone numbers and email addresses.

4. WORKING/NOT WORKING

This tool can be used to help a child/family think about and review from their perspective what is going well or 'working' and identify what is not working so well in their lives generally, and to identify support or care that is working well or highlight care that needs to be changed or improved. When things are not working well, it causes a child unnecessary upset or frustration.

It can be really helpful for a family to get other people's perspectives when considering what is working and not working for them. This may be achieved by involving someone else in care reviews/discussions, such as a family member or a close friend. The relationship circle helps to identify those trusted individuals who can provide objective views and support such situations.

First consider what is 'working' well with regard to care, support and life in general. Do the family or others need to do anything to ensure these things keep happening? Keep a note of any support that needs to remain unchanged. Then consider what is 'not working'. This helps to identify the care or support that may need to be modified or changed. Again, keep a note of this as you agree and update the care/support plan.

This is a useful tool or conversation for a family to use ahead of any appointments or review meetings with health care teams or other services, to help them focus and lead the conversation and ensure that things a child or family want to discuss or deal with remain on the agenda and do not get missed.

> Using this way of thinking makes us aware of what is working. We can then ensure we keep it in place. It also helps us clarify in our own minds what is not working. We then feel more able to identify the areas in which we need to ask for help when attending Hannah's reviews and appointments. (Rachel Tyler)

👍 Working	👎 Not working
Action: What I/we want or need to change:	

Example: A section of a 'Working/not working' document for Hannah, written by her mum to take to one of her multi-disciplinary (MDT) review meetings.

👍 Working	👎 Not working
Buggy: Buggy is really great and helps us get out and about.	Will soon outgrow current buggy and readjustment is needed.
Boots/splints: Boots and splints are fine. Understand ongoing arrangements for follow-up and ongoing support with Orthotics Department.	The toes on left foot are overlapping. Middle toenail is growing in a V shape and is sharp and difficult to cut.
Moving and handling: Building work is underway on new downstairs extension (bedroom and bathroom), which will help with moving and handling (no stairs to climb) and allow better facilities for short break support. Builder has recently been changed and progress is now being made.	Extension work has been fraught with problems and delays. Home hoist has been playing up. A sling assessment is required when the hoist is functional (OT aware). Our family have never had moving and handling training. Transferring in and out of the car is becoming more challenging. This needs consideration when Motability vehicle is changed. Car seat will soon need adjusting.

Short break support: Current home overnight short breaks service very helpful. The staff are really fantastic and allow Mum to catch up on some much needed sleep. Assessment has been made for contract care (24 nights away from home a year) but no family yet identified. Refer to Children's Hospice for short breaks support.	Three-hour home short breaks in daytime don't allow sufficient time to do anything really meaningful with sister, Lily. Hannah's sleep is easily disturbed at night. She does not always settle back to sleep if disturbed by overnight carers' checks. She is always best left to sleep and only disturbed when absolutely necessary – i.e. when responding to alarm, coughing or settling Hannah if distressed. Still waiting to find a family for 'out of home' short breaks on a regular basis for the next few years.
ENT (Ear, nose and throat):	Sleep apnoea continues. Date set for ENT review.
Dental support: Hannah goes to the family dentist.	H hates having her teeth brushed. We need to find the best way to protect her teeth.
Support at school: Support at school is absolutely brilliant. Teaching assistant fabulous.	It is difficult for Mum to work, due to taking H to school after late wake up on many mornings. There is no 'back-up plan' in place for days off school due to ill health, other than grandparents if they are free. A long-term solution would be useful.
Cleaning: Cleaning helps create time for the family.	It would be great if short breaks service could help with small tasks to support life at home – e.g. ironing.
Leisure/holidays: Enjoying all opportunities to socialise as a family and we love going away on holiday. H loves being entertained. She enjoys going out in her buggy on dog walks, playing with Stickle Bricks and swinging on her swing. H has a keen sense of humour and fun.	We would like to have a holiday away with friends, but due to high support needs we have not found a way to make this possible. 'Ad hoc' babysitting for both girls is difficult to organise. We rely heavily on grandparents. This will get more difficult in the future. This excludes us from some of the social activities we would like to join in with. Finding leisure activities that we can take part in as a family can prove very challenging. There are probably leisure facilities that we do not know about. Any help or ideas would be welcomed. Finding leisure activities to help H develop, learn and keep her body and mind active is challenging, especially in the school holidays.
Communication: H can communicate, if she is spoken to clearly, slowly, face to face, and given time to process questions or instructions (please see and use communication chart). The spoken word can be successfully backed up with the use of signing, pictures and Makaton symbols.	Ensuring H is receiving the correct help and support to assist communication and learning. It would be useful to explore if there are any further communication aids that could be used at home. H sometimes grabs and pulls and this can sometimes hurt those looking after her. How do we manage this safely and understand what H is trying to tell us?

5. ONE-PAGE PROFILES

A one-page profile is a summary of important information; describing what really matters to the child/young person and how to support them well. This is built up using all the information gathered with the child/family using person-centred tools and conversations such as 'important to/for,' 'working not working' and 'relationship circles'. Additional tools may also provide useful information, such as 'If I could I would' and 'communication charts'.

It is helpful to attach a photograph of the child to make the profile more personal. This should be quick and easy to read. It can be created as artistically as necessary to make it unique and to have the visual impact required. The key information will generally be:

- child's name and also what they like to be called

- date of birth

- people who are important to the child/young person

- what people have said they like and admire about the child/young person

- their hobbies and interests

- what the child likes and does not like

- how best to communicate with the child/young person if required

- a brief summary of their care and support – describing what good care looks like.

This information gathered and presented can be adapted as required to meet each individual's needs. Other details can be added if required, such as contact details, NHS number, etc.

We own the information about Hannah and our family and have been empowered to use it. We can update the information ourselves. (Rachel Tyler)

Example: One-page profile template

One-page profile

My name

I like to be known as

My birthday

Photograph

Important people to me:

What people like and admire about me:

My hobbies and interests. I enjoy:

I like:

I do not like:

Communicating with me:

My care and support needs:

Hannah's one-page profile

My name | **Hannah**

I like to be known as | **Han**

My birthday | **12 March 2003**

Photograph

Important people to me:

Mum, Dad, Sister Lily, Granny and Grandad, Barney our dog. Teaching assistant Janet, overnight short break carers (Ruth)

What people like and admire about me:

My relationship with dad, mum, sister and family

My personality and smile to melt your heart

My welcoming nature – a delight to be around

School wouldn't be school without me!

I enrich everyone's lives

I have a strong personality (and will be a strong woman!)

I am very affectionate with a wicked sense of humour!

My hobbies and interests. I enjoy:

Playing with Stickle Bricks

Looking at books and listening to stories

Going on dog walks in my buggy

Swinging on my swing seat in the garden

I like:

Routine, predictability and familiar adults

Being at home with my family and friends

Quiet time on my own

Stimulating activities at school and home

Being able to make choices

Being given some independence

I do not like:

Anything that is unexpected or unfamiliar

To be woken from sleep at any time day or night, as this can affect my breathing

When talking to me, please:

Make face contact and speak slowly, clearly and in short sentences

Give me at least 10 seconds to process what you have said

Do not keep repeating sentences

I understand Makaton and use visual symbols such as picture/photo cards

If you would like me to do something, say 'Hannah, do it' or 'It's time for...(bed, tea, etc.).'

My care and support needs:

If woken from sleep, day or night, I may have a 'floppy episode' and will need oxygen and my CPAP (continuous positive airway pressure). I have oxygen at night with an O2 saturation monitor. I use a salbutamol inhaler when I need help with breathing or have a cough. I have visual and hearing difficulties. I have glasses but do not like wearing them.

I use a buggy and walking frame to get around. I can also walk holding someone's hands. I have a tracking hoist at home. I wear orthotic boots/splints. I have a special sitting chair to help support me at the table at home/school. I have a special car seat. I wear a supportive hip brace at night. I have a special up/down bed and adapted bathroom. I have specialist ENT, neurology, respiratory and orthopaedic support.

OTHER PERSON-CENTRED TOOLS

There are a number of other useful person-centred tools or conversations which can help to support those receiving palliative care.

Each child and family is a unique individual. Person-centred tools and conversations can be used on 'pick and mix' basis, depending on a child and family's own situation. A handful of these tools are included in this guide, with examples to illustrate how they have been used in practice.

Person-centred approaches provide easy and practical ways to support staff and families and can also be used to think about their many roles in life, at home, school, work or in care settings.

- If I could I would…

- Communication charts

- What I want and do not want now and in the future – my hopes and fears

- My history…and my important memories

- Good day, bad day.

6. IF I COULD I WOULD (THE DREAM TOOL)

This conversation gives an opportunity for any individual or family to think about things they really want to achieve in their life – things they want to do or see, people they want to spend time with or places they want to visit. It may be things a family wants to do before their child dies. This conversation can help to assess an individual or family's view of their situation and how they are coping. This forms an important aspect of psychological, spiritual and social support in palliative care and helps to maintain hope.

This conversation should be framed carefully around each individual/ child/family and what they would like to achieve or what they want their life to look like. It may be that they have had broken sleep for months due to caring for a very ill child and would like to try to get a few peaceful nights' sleep each week. For those who have become isolated through ill-health or disability, it might mean getting out occasionally with friends or as a family. It may be wishing for a holiday if they are unable to get away due to circumstances. It may just be seeing their child maintaining a hobby or interest that makes them happy, such as swimming or riding for the disabled.

Example: Sherelle wrote her first 'If I could I would' for her daughter, Aria, aged almost three years. Good action planning meant these goals were achieved and new goals written and reviewed regularly. 'The dream conversation "If I could I would" gave us a chance to write down and work towards clear goals that we believed we could achieve' (Sherelle Ramus).

If I could I would...

> be at home to celebrate Christmas for the first time (not in hospital)
>
> stay well and keep out of hospital
>
> find ways to help others understand my communication better
>
> find better ways of getting around independently
>
> go to church every week with Mummy and Daddy
>
> go out more with my family and friends and visit my family in London
>
> find better ways to make my eczema more comfortable.

7. COMMUNICATION CHARTS

These charts are generally used to help children and young people who use non-verbal communication, such as behaviours, facial expressions and actions, to communicate. Understanding what a child is saying is a fundamental part of enabling and empowering them. It also ensures services are able to give effective support, especially those working closely with a child. Ask the family or carer to describe the different ways in which their child communicates, their facial expressions and behaviours and what they believe it means. Record how they respond and what should be done. This can help to identify pain/fear or discomfort and plan the necessary care/support required by the child.

This makes us and others really consider things from Hannah's perspective. (Rachel Tyler)

Where/when?	What happens?	We think it means...	And we should... (describe what you do)

Example: Hannah's communication chart.

Where/ when?	When H does this	We think it means...	And we should...
Anywhere or anytime	I do not appear to respond to what you are saying.	I am taking time to process and understand what you are saying.	When you speak to me or ask me questions, please make sure that you face me. Talk slowly, clearly and in short sentences to give me a better chance of understanding what you are saying. Please give me as many visual clues as you can. Use signing, pictures, Makaton symbols and show me objects.
			Please do not keep repeating what you are saying without a break. Say things once and allow me about 10 seconds' processing time. If you repeat things straight away, I have to start processing all over again!
			Please keep using the same words and sentences. I am very familiar with some sentences such as 'It's time for...' – e.g. 'It's time for bed', 'It's time for a bath', 'It's time for school'. If you want to encourage me to do something, say, 'Hannah, do it.'
			If you are going to do something to or with me, please tell me what you are going to do before you do it. Give me time to take in what you have said.
			I have some visual and hearing impairment and cannot always hear and see things clearly. I have glasses but don't like them on my face!
Anytime or anywhere	I give you a Makaton symbol or a picture.	I would like that particular object.	Please give me the object I have requested.
Anywhere or anytime	I pinch you, pull your clothes or hair.	I may be • tired • feeling crowded • frustrated • in discomfort • bored or have lost interest.	Move back a bit and let me have a bit of space. Sometimes I need 5–10 minutes quietly to myself. Please stay nearby so that you can see that I am safe but don't sit right next to me.

Situation	What I do	What it means	What you should do
After my bath in the evening	I pinch you or pull at you, at your clothes or hair.	It is probably because I am tired and it is 'time for bed'.	If it is before 6pm, please entertain me and keep me awake. If it is between 6 and 7pm you can get me ready for bed. My bedtime is 7pm if I can stay awake long enough.
At bedtime	I start shouting.	I may need the toilet or need changing. I may need some reassurance.	Please change me if necessary. Stay calm. Give me some quiet reassurance. Put on my coloured light, on the low setting.
Anytime	I look at a drink you are offering me.	It often means that I may like a drink.	Wait patiently to see if I want a drink. Don't rush me. Offer me a choice of drinks please. Use words and Makaton symbols for milk, juice or water. Wait for me to choose which one, give me time to think.
	I push a drink away quite quickly.	I don't want a drink.	Be prepared for me to push the drink away if I do not want it. Please hold the cup for me. Be prepared, I may knock it out of your hand. I think it's funny if you get wet!
Anytime or anywhere	I put my head down so that you can't see my face.	I may be crying as I am in pain. Or I am upset because: • you have taken something away from me that I want • there is loud noise that I don't like • someone else is upset/ crying.	Please sit me on your knee and give me a cuddle and reassure me.
Around mealtimes	I shuffle to my chair at the table and try to sit in it.	I am hungry…or thirsty.	Please get my lunch or tea ready!
Mealtimes	I push my plate or bowl away.	I am not ready to eat. The food is too hot for me.	Remove the food/bowl/plate or be ready to catch my bowl in case I decide to throw it! Please also make sure that the chair next to me is out of my reach as I like to push it over! Please don't crowd me at the table – I am quite happy to eat by myself.
When playing anytime	I throw my toys.	I don't want to play with them anymore.	Let me play with one thing at a time. Give me time and my own space. When I am ready, I will seek you out and might want to sit on your knee.

Example: Sherelle wrote this communication chart for her daughter, Aria, to take with her on first day at school.

When this happens	We think it means	We need you to do this	Medication Please follow my medicine chart
When I'm sitting down or lying down I keep trying to pull myself up.	I want to get up. I want to stand on my feet.	Help me up on to my feet. It's better if you put me in my support shoes to do this.	Glycopyrronium Bromide (1mg in 5mls) (5mls before feed) (to reduce my saliva) Gaviscon (dissolve ½ sachet in each feed) (to reduce tummy acid) Chlorphenamine (4mg tablet) give me ¼ tablet dissolved in 3mls water (for allergic reactions) Calpol (120mg in 5mls sugar-free) give 8mls or Nurofen (100mg in 5mls sugar-free) give 5mls (to help me with pain) Buccal Midazolam 5mg in ready loaded syringe (please follow my seizure emergency care plan) Melatonin (1mg in 1ml) give me 2mls PRN (to help me sleep at night)
I flap my hands, start crying. I puff up my face/cheeks.	I am trying to go to the toilet. I'm probably constipated.	Help me by giving me something to push my feet against. When I'm lying on my back and I start pushing, you can gently push my knees up towards my chest (please don't push too hard).	

Symptoms	What I'm telling you	What to do	Additional information
I keep crying and appear frustrated.	1. I'm tired. 2. I'm struggling to go to the toilet. 3. I want to move from this chair or position. 4. I am in pain. 5. I feel unwell. 6. I may be de-saturating and need oxygen.	1. Help me to get comfortable, play some music. 2. Help me by giving me something to push my feet against to help me go to the toilet. I take 10 mls Lactulose (3.35g per 5ml) am/pm. 3. Move me to a different position or cuddle me. 4. Check my temperature and give sugar-free pain relief prescribed on medicine chart. 5. Check my temperature and give sugar-free medication to reduce my temperature as prescribed on medicine chart. 6. Check my O2 saturation level, give me oxygen 0.05–0.1 litres from portable cylinder until I settle.	**Eczema Creams (See Medicine Chart)** Hydromol and Aveeno (*used daily on my face and body*) Dermovate steroid cream and Protopic cream (*only if my eczema flares up*) **Things that calm me** I love my music. I also like singing and cuddles. **Please Remember** If I am ill I sometimes desaturate during the day. Check my oxygen (O2) using my saturation monitor. If below 92% you will need to connect me to a portable O2 cylinder at 0.05–0.1 litres. **Every night** I have O2 via nasal cannulae from my oxygen concentrator 0.05–0.1 litres.
• I keep rolling my head. • I am unsettled. • My neck is pink with lots of bumps. • Constant head and neck turning.	1. I'm tired. 2. My body is itching (eczema). 3. I am having an allergic reaction.	1. Help me to get comfortable. 2. Place eczema cream on my body & spray on my head. Put on scratch mittens so I don't hurt myself. 3. Give me Chlorphenamine ¼ of a 4mg tablet (dissolve ¼ tablet in 3 mls water) & put down my gastrostomy mini button with 10 mls flush (follow medicine chart).	**WARNING:** I am on a strict **Ketogenic Diet.** I do not take sugar/carbohydrates. **Please DO NOT give me anything other than the food my mum provides. Mum checks ketone levels weekly using a monitor.** **Solids (Ketogenic Diet)** If I eat all my food I only need ½ my milk. If I do not eat you will need to carefully judge how much milk to give me.
• I look vacant and non-responsive. • I am lip smacking. • Convulsions.	I am having a seizure.	Please follow my emergency care plan which contains seizure care instructions.	**Milk (Ketogenic Diet)** via Gastrostomy using my **Homeward feeding pump** Pump settings: Dose=155 & Rate=310 **Gravity feed** when I am well=100mls milk then make up to 175mls by adding water.

8. WHAT I WANT AND DO NOT WANT NOW AND IN THE FUTURE – MY HOPES AND FEARS

This conversation is really useful for planning ahead and thinking about what an individual, child, young person and/or their family would love to achieve or to happen in the future. What would they like to happen to them if they had a choice? This may be who they want to care for them. It may be where they want to be cared for now and in the future, especially at end of life. It involves discussing what the child/family would like to avoid happening. This is a great conversation and particularly relevant during advance care planning discussions or during the transition of a young person with life-threatening illness who is reaching the age of 18 and moving into adulthood. It is a simple tool to use.

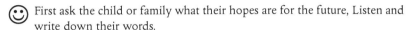 First ask the child or family what their hopes are for the future, Listen and write down their words.

Then ask about their fears or concerns for the future. This is a great way to find out if future hopes seem realistic. Ensure that children and families are made aware of all the options available to them so that they can identify achievable goals or outcomes.

> This conversation gave us opportunity to plan ahead and, at any one point in time, we would think about what was important to us now and in the future. We were able to express our hopes and our fears. (Sherelle Ramus)

Example: At the end of her treatment for cancer, Emma, who was 16 years of age, described what she was planning now and in the future – she discussed her hopes and fears.

🙂 Hopes	☹ Fears
No more treatment (I can't remember what life was like before treatment).	I am scared about finishing treatment. This has been my life for the last two years – what will happen next? Cancer could come back.
Not to wear my wig anymore. I would like help to find a new hairstyle that works for me.	
That I stop feeling tired and worn out all the time.	Taking my wig off. My hair has grown back and feels different and I don't really like it.
To feel more confident in myself.	Tiredness carrying on.
To get back to school and catch up with school work and take my mocks and GCSEs in science, maths, English, health studies and social care.	Talking to my mum about how I feel – if I am feeling down or upset, I know it worries her.
Go to sixth form college to study childcare.	I won't make it to school as much as I need to, and may not pass my exams.

9. MY HISTORY...AND MY IMPORTANT MEMORIES

This is a way of recording significant or special events that have happened in a person's life. It is a way of recording treasured memories. It can save families repeating information many times to different services. This history may contain details of health, education, social and leisure events. Building a record of treasured events and memories is valuable for families with a child receiving palliative care and also for families receiving bereavement support. There are many other creative ways to record memories – for example, on posters, on film or in photograph albums, in a journal, in a memory box, or by making hand- and footprints.

Example: Sherelle wrote this history and memories for her daughter, Aria, for family and services to read, along with a detailed relationship circle. 'This is useful because we don't have to repeat history again and again – it is written down for anyone to read' (Sherelle Ramus).

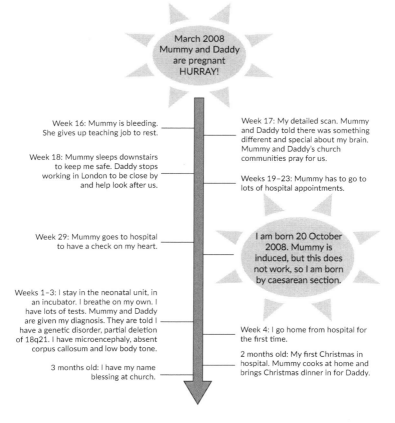

March 2008 Mummy and Daddy are pregnant HURRAY!

Week 16: Mummy is bleeding. She gives up teaching job to rest.

Week 17: My detailed scan. Mummy and Daddy told there was something different and special about my brain. Mummy and Daddy's church communities pray for us.

Week 18: Mummy sleeps downstairs to keep me safe. Daddy stops working in London to be close by and help look after us.

Weeks 19–23: Mummy has to go to lots of hospital appointments.

Week 29: Mummy goes to hospital to have a check on my heart.

I am born 20 October 2008. Mummy is induced, but this does not work, so I am born by caesarean section.

Weeks 1–3: I stay in the neonatal unit, in an incubator. I breathe on my own. I have lots of tests. Mummy and Daddy are given my diagnosis. They are told I have a genetic disorder, partial deletion of 18q21. I have microencephaly, absent corpus callosum and low body tone.

Week 4: I go home from hospital for the first time.

2 months old: My first Christmas in hospital. Mummy cooks at home and brings Christmas dinner in for Daddy.

3 months old: I have my name blessing at church.

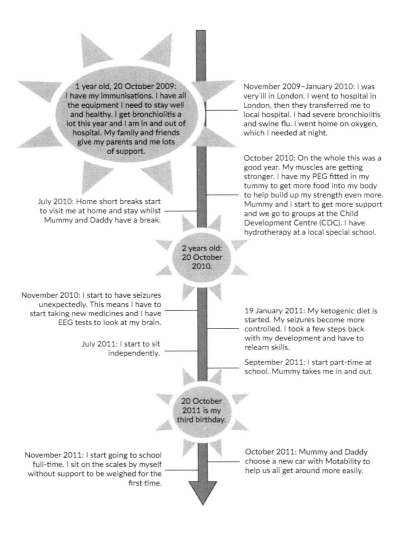

1 year old, 20 October 2009: I have my immunisations. I have all the equipment I need to stay well and healthy. I get bronchiolitis a lot this year and I am in and out of hospital. My family and friends give my parents and me lots of support.

November 2009–January 2010: I was very ill in London. I went to hospital in London, then they transferred me to local hospital. I had severe bronchiolitis and swine flu. I went home on oxygen, which I needed at night.

October 2010: On the whole this was a good year. My muscles are getting stronger. I have my PEG fitted in my tummy to get more food into my body to help build up my strength even more. Mummy and I start to get more support and we go to groups at the Child Development Centre (CDC). I have hydrotherapy at a local special school.

July 2010: Home short breaks start to visit me at home and stay whilst Mummy and Daddy have a break.

2 years old: 20 October 2010.

November 2010: I start to have seizures unexpectedly. This means I have to start taking new medicines and I have EEG tests to look at my brain.

19 January 2011: My ketogenic diet is started. My seizures become more controlled. I took a few steps back with my development and have to relearn skills.

July 2011: I start to sit independently.

September 2011: I start part-time at school. Mummy takes me in and out.

20 October 2011 is my third birthday.

November 2011: I start going to school full-time. I sit on the scales by myself without support to be weighed for the first time.

October 2011: Mummy and Daddy choose a new car with Motability to help us all get around more easily.

10. GOOD DAY/BAD DAY

This is another conversation that helps to gather unique information and can be used to identify things that are important to and important for a person. All of us have good days and bad days. It can be helpful to listen to what makes a really good day for a child and/or family and what happens when bad days occur.

Discuss what makes a good day for the child/family. Is there anything you or others could do to help good days happen more often?

Now think about what happens on a bad day. Is there anything that you or others could do to prevent bad days happening, or make them happen less often?

☀ Good day	☁ Bad day
What I/we want to change…	

Example: Good day/bad day for James written with the care team and James during a short break at a children's hospice.

☀ Good day	☁ Bad day
• I like to be involved and in the middle of any activity, especially with my friends or other young people, particularly those my own age. • Being spoken to and able to make choices. • Taking chill-out time when I get tired and need a rest. • Please look at my **communication chart** to find out the best ways to talk to me and understand what I am saying to you.	• Being 'parked' somewhere in my wheelchair. • Not involved, being left on my own without anyone or anything to do.
• Feeling well so I can enjoy the day and activities planned for me. • Comfortable and free from pain – please use my **communication chart** to understand how I tell you that I am uncomfortable or in pain. Please use my **care plan and medication chart** to help manage my pain.	• Feeling poorly. • Being uncomfortable or in pain.
• Able to enjoy sensory activities and other pastimes that I enjoy such as listening to music, watching music videos and watching TV (especially the soaps).	• Being left without any sensory activities to enjoy.

ACKNOWLEDGEMENTS

1. AUTHORS

Rebecca Riley (RGN, RSCN, District Nurse, MA, PG CERT in personal and business coaching) has worked in a number of clinical nurse specialist roles including that of Cystic Fibrosis Nurse Specialist, Macmillan Nurse and manager of a children's cancer unit, and as Lead Officer of a children's hospice. In 2008 she established a small company offering organisational development (OD) support, training and coaching services. Becca has a special interest in working with children and young people with long-term conditions and complex health care needs, their families and the services that support them. Becca has coached children, young people and families living with long-term illness to help them with decision making, to deal with the changes they face in their lives and to empower them, putting them in the driving seat. She uses a wide range of approaches to support her work, particularly those based in person-centred practice (PCP). Becca has been Practitioner Health Lecturer in Children's Palliative Care at the University of Nottingham; she is a Specialist Advisor for Care Quality Commission (CQC) in end-of-life care and a Clinical Associate for Gold Standards Framework (GSF). She is an active member of the East Midlands Children's and Young People's Palliative Care Network (EMCYPPCN) and a member of the faculty at East Midlands Leadership Academy.

Rachel Tyler has been trained in using person-centred planning (PCP) and has helped develop this guidance from a parental perspective. Rachel wears many hats. She once described herself as a Mum, Wife, Expert parent-carer, Lawyer, Household administrator and manager! She says: 'I attended a two-day person-centred planning programme with my twin daughters about six years ago. We were introduced to a range of person-centred planning tools and conversations, alongside other families and some of the services that supported our family. We have since had experience of using many of these tools in our daily lives. Some of the examples I have included demonstrate the useful person-centred conversations we have had and the records we have made, and explain why person-centred planning has helped us. I hope they help to illustrate how person-centred thinking and planning can build up a more complete picture of a child or family in the world in which they live and belong and where care and support will take place on a daily basis.'

Sherelle Ramus was trained in person-centred planning (PCP) and started to use some of these approaches when her eldest daughter, Aria, was three years old and about to start attending special school. Aria was born with a complex genetic disorder and as a baby her health was unstable and management was challenging. 'PCP increased our confidence to talk to the many different services we received support from and allowed us to take more ownership as a family. PCP is now common language in many different services and as a family we have shared person-centred information to support our daughter at school and with home short breaks carers. The information we recorded also supported us through adoption processes. We saved all this information on our computer and can easily update it ourselves as and when needed. We have had some useful and challenging conversations and using person-centred approaches enabled us to take time to reflect and think through many challenges in a different way, often finding creative solutions. We hope this guide helps others to do the same.'

2. CONTRIBUTORS AND SUPPORTERS

Dr Lynda Brook, Macmillan Consultant in Paediatric Palliative Care, Alder Hey Specialist Palliative Care team, is a firm believer in person-centred planning (PCP). Her ongoing support and input over a number of years is greatly appreciated to help achieve this written PCP guidance, for children and young people receiving palliative/end-of-life care, their families and the services who support them.

In 2012 **Sacha Langton-Gilks's** son, David (known as DD), died peacefully and happily at home of a brain tumour, aged 16. The local GP's surgery had been through Gold Standards Framework (GSF) training in end-of-life care and provided the family with excellent coordination of care between the hospital and the community care teams. Sacha is a singing teacher, gardener and writer. She is also a Lead Champion for the HeadSmart campaign. Sacha spoke publicly to other parents, at the request of the Brain Tumour Charity, about the process of managing DD's death at home. This was in response to the needs of families in the end-of-life phase, who had said they did not receive information and felt isolated. She has since presented to health professionals at a Gold Standards Framework event and was asked to write her experiences down – hence the publication of this book.

Sarah Everest, NHS Commissioner and Registered Children's Nurse, has supported the development of this guidance and the ongoing person-centred work with families, for which we are very grateful. She says: 'This guide is a really useful and practical tool for families and professionals to use for person-centred planning in their everyday life. Being developed by parent-experts and a health professional with years of experience and a passion for person-centred planning ensures it is a simple and easy-to-use guide. People can feel daunted by new initiatives such as PCP and may think that this is time-consuming and complicated. This guide contains lots of useful tools and examples that can be used regularly in practice to support families and ensure that their child is kept at the centre of integrated care provision. I hope many families and professionals will benefit from the use of this excellent guide and toolkit.'

Together for Short Lives have supported the development of this guidance. Examples in it have been shared at Together for Short Lives national events to support integrated education, health and care (EHC) planning. The charity has a wonderful website, which is extremely helpful. Please follow the link to the TfSL's website to find resources and information to support families and professionals: www.togetherforshortlives.org.uk.

The team at **Gold Standards Framework** has been very supportive of the work to develop this document. We hope this guidance encompasses the ethos of GSF, in promoting person-centred thinking and practice to help promote 'Living well' and 'Dying well'.

Thanks go to **Dr Sue Neilson**, Lecturer, School of Nursing, University of Birmingham, for her support in the development of this guidance and for securing a funded research evaluation of the person-centred toolkit in practice. Sue's research interest in children and young people's (CYP) palliative care has been informed by over 20 years' clinical nursing experience in this field.

We are so very grateful to **Clare Periton**, Chief Executive and **Dr Emily Harrop**, Consultant in Paediatric Palliative Care, both from Helen and Douglas House Hospice, for their contributions to the foreword of the Person-Centred guidance and for their on-going support and encouragement with the development of this resource and in aligning its application to best practice as described in the NICE guidance on End of Life Care for Infants, children and young people with life limiting conditions: Planning and management (NG 61).

BIBLIOGRAPHY

Department of Health (2008) *Better Care: Better Lives. Improving Outcomes and Experiences for Children, Young People and Their Families Living with Life-Limiting and Life-Threatening Conditions.* London: Department of Health.

Department of Health (2010) 'End of life care planning with people who have a personal health budget.' Discussion paper produced by the Department of Health's personal health budgets pilot programme and the NHS National End of Life Care programme. London: Department of Health.

Department of Health (2010a) *Personalisation through Person-Centred Planning.* London: Department of Health.

National Institute for Health and Care Excellence (NICE) (2016) End of Life care for infants, children and young people with life-limiting conditions: planning and management, NICE guideline. www.nice.org.uk/guidance/ng61/resources/end-of-life-care-for-infants-children-and-young-people-withlifelimiting-conditions-planning-and-management-1837568722885.

National Institute for Health and Care Excellence (NICE) (2017) End of life care for infants, children and young people Quality standard [QS160]. www.nice.org.uk/guidance/qs160/history.

O'Brien, J. and Lovett, H. (1992) 'Finding a Way toward Everyday Lives: The Contribution of Person-Centred Planning.' In J. O'Brien and C.O. O'Brien (eds) *A Little Book about Person-Centred Planning.* Toronto: Inclusion Press.

Ritchie, P., Sanderson, H., Kilbane, J. and Routledge, M. (2003) *People, Plans and Practicalities: Achieving Change through Person Centred Planning.* Edinburgh: SHS Trust.

Sanderson, H. (2000) *Person-Centered Planning: Key Features and Approaches.* York: Joseph Rowntree Foundation.

Sanderson, H. and Lewis, J. (2011) *A Practical Guide to Delivering Personalisation: Person-Centred Practice in Health and Social Care.* London: Jessica Kingsley Publishers.

The Health Foundation (2014) *Person-Centred Care Made Simple: What Everyone Should Know about Person-Centred Care.* London: The Health Foundation.

Together for Short Lives (2017) Palliative care definitions. Accessed on 27/06/17 at www.togetherforshortlives.org.uk.

Wolfensberger, W. (1972) *The Principle of Normalization in Human Services.* Toronto: National Institute on Mental Retardation.

RESOURCES

Chambers, L. and Taylor, V. (2014) *A Family Companion to the Together for Short Lives Core Care Pathway for Children with Life-limiting and Life-threatening Conditions* (3rd edition). Bristol: Together for Short Lives.

Helen Sanderson Associates (2010) *Living Well: Thinking and Planning for the End of Your Life.* Stockport: HSA Press.

Helen Sanderson Associates – Please do visit the Helen Sanderson Associates website where you will find a wide range of useful tools and resources to support person-centred planning: http://helensandersonassociates.co.uk/person-centred-practice/person-centred-thinking-tools

Sanderson, H. and Taylor, M. (2008) *Celebrating Families: Simple, Practical Ways to Enhance Family Life.* Stockport: HSA Press.

Together for Short Lives is the leading UK charity for all children with life-threatening and life-limiting conditions and all those who support, love and care for them – families, professionals and services. Do visit the Together for Short Lives website where you will find a comprehensive collection of resources and information: www.togetherforshortlives.org.uk.

Index